I, _____, IN DEVOTION

BOTH TO THE WILL OF GOD AND TO THIS NATION

THAT HE HAS BLESSED SO RICHLY, DO HEREBY PLEDGE

TO PRAY DAILY FOR THE PRESIDENT OF THE

UNITED STATES AND FOR THE OTHER LEADERS

OF MY NATION AND COMMUNITY.

SIGNATURE: _____

DATE: _____

To register your membership on *The Presidential Prayer Team* and
receive a membership decal and weekly prayer updates, go to
www.presidentialprayerteam.org.

Blessed is the nation whose God is the LORD.

—PSALM 33:12

You will pray to Him, and He will hear you, and you will fulfill your vows.
What you decide will be done, and light will shine on your ways.

—JOB 22:27–28 (NIV)

THE
PRESIDENTIAL
PRAYER TEAM

Devotional

J COUNTRYMAN®

Nashville, Tennesse

Contributing writer: Meagan Gillan
Project editor: Kathy Baker
Associate editor: Michelle Orr

www.thomasnelson.com
www.jcountryman.com

www.presidentialprayerteam.org
www.presidentialprayerkids.org

Designed by Kirk DouPonce, interior by Robin Black, UDG|Designworks, Sisters, Oregon

Cover art, "Prayer Over the White House" by C. Michael Dudash

ISBN: 1-4041-0080-6

Printed and bound in the United States of America

WE ALL CAN PRAY. WE ALL SHOULD PRAY.

WE SHOULD ASK THE FULFILLMENT OF GOD'S WILL.

WE SHOULD ASK FOR COURAGE, WISDOM,

FOR THE QUIETNESS OF SOUL

WHICH COMES ALONE TO THEM

WHO PLACE THEIR LIVES IN HIS HANDS.

—PRESIDENT HARRY S. TRUMAN

We the People *of the United States...*

www.presidentialprayerteam.org.

CONTENTS

★ ★ ★

Introduction—*The President & Other Leaders Need Our Prayers* 9

Chapter One—*Our Nation's Godly Heritage* 13

Chapter Two—*Praying Affects My Heart, Home, Nation, & World* . . 47

Chapter Three—*How & What We Need to Pray* 85

Chapter Four—*Our Nation's Godly Future* 111

Conclusion—*I Will Pray for the Leaders of Today . . . and Tomorrow* . . 131

About *The Presidential Prayer Team* 134

Scriptures About Prayer 138

Acknowledgments 142

We had spoken to the king, saying,
"The hand of our God is upon all those for good
who seek Him, but His power and His wrath are against all
those who forsake Him." So we fasted and entreated
our God for this, and He answered our prayer.

—EZRA 8:22–23

THE PRESIDENT & OTHER LEADERS NEED OUR PRAYERS

★ ★ ★

*J*ust a simple idea . . . with an immeasurable impact: Mobilize Americans to pray.

A new chapter is being written in the history of the United States of America. People are experiencing a strong sense of unity and purpose. *The Presidential Prayer Team* is part of that, encouraging Americans to unite further through the practice of daily prayer for the President, for the Cabinet, and for other leaders of our nation. More than two million people already have made that commitment, and this nonpolitical effort will continue regardless of who is elected to the presidency, because we know the strength and courage that comes from being a nation that prays.

No one can estimate the influence this mighty prayer effort has had on our President and our country, but the universal enthusiasm for this spiritual movement is a testimony to the faith and character of the American people.

The Presidential Prayer Team started simply, with one person, just as so many of this nation's great movements have begun. Sculptor and inventor William Hunter minted a special coin and gave it away to friends and associates as a reminder to uphold our President in prayer. They soon requested more to pass along to others. Over time, he envisioned a nationwide prayer effort for the President. Dr. Cornell "Corkie" Haan, a national facilitator with Mission America, joined Hunter in this founding effort of *The Presidential Prayer Team*.

They planned to launch the effort in November of 2001. Then the September 11th terrorist attacks occurred, and it became clear that this prayer effort was primed by God to be ready for such a time. The staff worked around the clock to complete the website and all of the other pieces of the organizational puzzle within days. Positive response to the effort was immediate and overwhelming, as tens of thousands of people began signing up daily via the Internet and telephone.

And the wave of support is still growing.

Leaders today, especially the President of the United States, confront challenges the nation's founders never could have imagined. Our leaders cannot rely on human wisdom alone as they cope with the myriad complexities of the twenty–first century. They must connect with the holy Source of supernatural wisdom. They must pray.

And our leaders can't carry this burden alone. If we are truly patriotic—and faithful—we must pray, too.

As you read this devotional, may you realize anew the power of your prayers. The President, Vice President, Cabinet, and other leaders make decisions that influence every level of our lives—from what local services are available to what issues are discussed on the national agenda—so praying for them is essential. Their decisions impact our homes, our communities, our nation, and our world. We must pray that their decisions benefit this country and, most of all, God's Kingdom.

We must pray.

My family and I have been blessed by the prayers of countless Americans. We have felt their sustaining power and we're incredibly grateful. Tremendous challenges await this nation, and there will be hardships ahead. Faith will not make our path easy, but it will give us strength for the journey.

—PRESIDENT GEORGE W. BUSH

WE HAVE NO GOVERNMENT ARMED

WITH POWER CAPABLE OF CONTENDING WITH

HUMAN PASSIONS UNBRIDLED BY MORALITY AND

RELIGION. AVARICE, AMBITION, REVENGE,

OR GALLANTRY WOULD BREAK THE STRONGEST

CORDS OF OUR CONSTITUTION

AS A WHALE GOES THROUGH A NET. OUR

CONSTITUTION WAS MADE ONLY FOR A MORAL AND

RELIGIOUS PEOPLE. IT IS WHOLLY INADEQUATE TO

THE GOVERNMENT OF ANY OTHER.

—President John Adams

Chapter One

★ ★ ★

OUR NATION'S GODLY HERITAGE

The United States was founded on faith—faith that in the New World, people could worship freely and the poor and oppressed could flourish. Faith that in the New World life would be better. Freer. New.

The faith had a primary name—Christianity, a religion centered on personal preparation for life in the new, eternal world still to come. Our founders' individual views of the Christian faith varied greatly, and although we now reject some of their practices, such as slaveholding, we must not deny their essential belief system.

Patriot Patrick Henry said, "It cannot be emphasized too strongly or too often that this great nation was founded, not by religionists, but by Christians; not on religions, but on the Gospel of Jesus Christ."

Certainly, the New World on earth was not a perfect world—the shame of our nation's history is how many generations suffered before all people were welcome to participate in freedom's opportunities—but no other people on earth have ever enjoyed such blessing. From Christopher Columbus's 1493 letter announcing his discovery, to the Declaration of Independence, the Articles of Confederation, and the Constitution, our founding documents all acknowledge those blessings or the Source of those blessings.

And no other people have ever shared those blessings so freely. For instance, the most–loved portion of the poem at the Statue of Liberty is beautifully similar to a treasured promise of Jesus:

*"Come to Me, all you who labor
and are heavy laden,
and I will give you rest."*
—LUKE 11:28

*Give me your tired, your poor,
Your huddled masses yearning
to breathe free,
The wretched refuse of your
teeming shore,
Send these, the homeless,
tempest-tost to me,
I lift my lamp beside the
golden door.*
—EMMA LAZARUS

So revisit our nation's godly heritage. Refresh your appreciation of the founding principles. Renew your commitment to pray as our early leaders prayed.

Of all the dispositions and habits which lead to political prosperity, religion and morality are indispensable supports. . . . And let us with caution indulge the supposition that morality can be maintained without religion. Whatever may be conceded to the influence of refined education on minds of peculiar structure, reason and experience both forbid us to expect that national morality can prevail in exclusion of religious principle. . . .

Though, in reviewing the incidents of my administration, I am unconscious of intentional error, I am nevertheless too sensible of my defects not to think it probable that I may have committed many errors. Whatever they may be, I fervently beseech the Almighty to avert or mitigate the evils to which they may tend. I shall also carry with me the hope that my country will never cease to view them with indulgence; and that, after forty five years of my life dedicated to its service with an upright zeal, the faults of incompetent abilities will be consigned to oblivion, as myself must soon be to the mansions of rest.

—President George Washington
In His Farewell Address, 1796

'WE ARE A CHRISTIAN PEOPLE'

★ ★ ★

*M*any years ago I was encouraged to learn of the overwhelming historical evidence that commitment to Christ and biblical Christianity were the driving forces behind the founding of America.

For example, in 1607, when the first permanent English–speaking settlers in America landed on the coast of Virginia, their first act was to plant a cross and dedicate this new continent to God Almighty.

A few years later in 1620, the settlers at Plymouth made a covenant with God called the Mayflower Compact. It stated, "In the name of God . . . Having undertaken for the glory of God and advancement of the Christian faith . . in the presence of God and one another, covenant and combine ourselves into a civil body politic."

The Delaware Constitution, typical of the other colonies, declared that a candidate for office must say: "I do profess faith in God the Father, and in Jesus Christ his only Son, and in the Holy Ghost. In God who is blessed forevermore I do acknowledge the Holy Scriptures and the Old and New Testaments which are given by divine inspiration."

Most of the original signers of the Constitution were not deists as some historians claim. Research has proven that the vast majority were avowed, Bible-believing Christians.

The father of our country, President George Washington, said:

- "To the distinguished Character of a Patriot, it should be our highest glory to add the most distinguished Character of Christian."

- "Bless O Lord the whole race of mankind, and let the world be filled with the knowledge of Thee and Thy Son, Jesus Christ."

- "It is impossible to rightly govern the world without God and the Bible."

- "Of all the habits which lead to political prosperity, religion and morality are indispensable supports . . . Reason and experience both forbid us to expect that national morality can prevail in exclusion of religious principle."

Patrick Henry, an American revolutionary leader, said, "It cannot be emphasized too strongly or too often that this great nation was founded, not by religionists, but by Christians; not on religions, but on the Gospel of Jesus Christ."

Sixth President John Quincy Adams said, "The highest glory of the American Revolution was this: It connected, in one indissoluble bond, the principles of civil government and the principles of Christianity."

An extensive study and report by the U. S. House Committee on the Judiciary declared in 1854: "At the time of the adoption of the Constitution and the amendments, the universal sentiment was that Christianity . . . must be considered as the foundation on which the whole structure rests. . . . That was the religion of the founders of the republic, and they expected it to remain the religion of their descendants."

In 1892, the U.S. Supreme Court studied our history and concluded, "We are a Christian people . . . These, and many other matters which might be noticed, add a volume of unofficial declarations to the mass of organic utterances that this is a Christian nation" *(The Church of the Holy Trinity v. United States)*.

As recently as 1931, the U.S. Supreme Court declared, "We are a Christian people" *(United States v. Macintosh)*.

By God's grace, in spite of our personal and national sins, for which we must repent, America is the most blessed, most powerful, most free and greatest missionary–sending nation in history.

DR. BILL BRIGHT
Founder, President and Chairman Emeritus
Campus Crusade for Christ International
& Honorary Committee Member
of *The Presidential Prayer Team*

"AS OUR NATION FACES A TROUBLED

AND UNCERTAIN FUTURE,

IT IS MORE IMPERATIVE THAN EVER

THAT WE CONTINUE TO UPHOLD IT, AND OUR

PRESIDENT, IN FERVENT PRAYER. IT IS THE

RESPONSIBILITY AND PRIVILEGE OF

EVERY CHRISTIAN IN AMERICA."

—BILL BRIGHT

A FOUNDER'S FAITH: ROGER SHERMAN

★ ★ ★

*R*oger Sherman was one of the most significant of all our Founding Fathers. A delegate to the Continental Congress from Connecticut, he was the only man who signed all four of the great state papers: the Articles of Association of 1774, the Declaration of Independence, the Articles of Confederation, and the Constitution.

When the Continental Congress struggled to know how to give fair representation to the smaller states as well as the large ones, it was Sherman who broke the impasse with the suggestion that the Congress be composed of two bodies—one, the Senate, giving equal representation to every state, and another, the House of Representatives, giving more representatives to larger states, depending on population. His proposal, which some credit with saving the Constitutional Convention from collapse, was called the "Connecticut Compromise."

Sherman helped draft the Declaration of Independence and the Bill of Rights, and he was referred to by Patrick Henry as one of the three greatest men at the Constitutional Convention.

More importantly, Roger Sherman was a theologian. When asked by his pastor in 1788 to use his knowledge to revise the belief statement of his local church, he penned a lengthy statement that clearly defines his steadfast belief in the God of the Bible. Here is a portion of his creed: *"I believe that there is one only living and true God, existing in three persons, the Father, the Son, and the Holy Ghost, the same in substance equal in power and glory. That the Scriptures of the Old and New Testaments are a revelation from God, and a complete rule to direct us how we may glorify and enjoy Him."*

OPENING WITH PRAYER & SCRIPTURE

★ ★ ★

Though there are countless examples of the godly heritage of our Founding Fathers, this simple letter from John Adams to his wife, Abigail, may express, as well as any other early American document, the spirit of prayer, faith, and godliness that prevailed among the Fathers as they met during those early days of the Constitutional Convention. Adams, a signer of the Declaration of Independence, our first Vice President and our second President, regularly wrote his reflections to his wife. September 7, 1774 was the first day of the first session of the Continental Congress in Philadelphia. He recalls the events of the day in this letter to Abigail, who remained at the family homestead near Boston, Massachusetts. This letter makes clear how commonplace the reading of Scripture and the reliance on prayer were to our nation's founders. To them it was a welcome and cherished part of every day.

"When the Congress met, Mr. Cushing made a motion that it should be opened with prayer. It was opposed . . . because we were so divided in religious sentiments, some Episcopalians, some Quakers, some Anabaptists, some Presbyterians, and some Congregationalists, that we could not join in the same act of worship. Mr. Samuel Adams arose and said that he was no bigot, and could hear a prayer from any gentleman of piety and virtue, who was at the same time a friend to his country. He moved that Mr. Duché, an Episcopal clergyman might . . . read prayers to Congress tomorrow morning.

The motion was passed in the affirmative. The next morning, [Rev. Duché] appeared . . . and read several prayers in the established form, and read for

the seventh day of September, which was the thirty–fifth Psalm. You must remember, this was the next morning after we heard the horrible rumor of the cannonade of Boston.

I never saw a greater effect upon an audience. It seemed as if heaven had ordained that Psalm to be read on that morning. After this, Mr. Duché, unexpectedly to everybody, struck out into an extemporary prayer, which filled the bosom of every man present. I must confess, I never heard a better prayer, or one so well pronounced. It has had an excellent effect upon everybody here. I must beg you to read that Psalm."

A Portion of the First Prayer in Congress

O Lord our Heavenly Father, high and mighty King of kings, and Lord of lords, who dost from Thy throne behold all the dwellers on earth and reignest with power supreme and uncontrolled over all the Kingdoms, Empires and Governments; look down in mercy, we beseech Thee, on these our American States, who have fled to Thee from the rod of the oppressor and thrown themselves on Thy gracious protection, desiring to be henceforth dependent only on Thee, to Thee have they appealed for the righteousness of their cause; to Thee do they now look up for that countenance and support, which Thou alone canst give; take them, therefore, Heavenly Father, under Thy nurturing care; give them wisdom in council and valor in the field; defeat the malicious designs of our cruel adversaries; convince them of the unrighteousness of their cause, and if they persist in their sanguinary purposes, of own unerring justice, sounding in their hearts, constrain them to drop the weapons of war from their unnerved bands in the day of battle! Be Thou present, O God of wisdom, and direct the councils of this honorable assembly; enable them to settle things on the best and surest foundation.

—September 7, 1774 by Jacob Duché

We the People of the United States...

GRACIOUS GOD, ALL THAT WE HAVE

AND ARE IS A RESULT OF YOUR AMAZING

GENEROSITY. SINCE SEPTEMBER 11TH, IN THE BATTLE

AGAINST TERRORISM, WE HAVE DISCOVERED

AGAIN THAT YOU TRULY ARE OUR REFUGE

AND STRENGTH, AN EVER-PRESENT HELP IN TROUBLE.

WE REDEDICATE OURSELVES TO THE

ONE NATION UNDER YOU. IN YOU WE TRUST.

WE REAFFIRM OUR ACCOUNTABILITY TO YOU, TO THE

ABSOLUTES OF YOUR COMMANDMENTS,

AND TO JUSTICE IN OUR SOCIETY. BLESS OUR

PRESIDENT, CONGRESS, AND ALL OUR LEADERS WITH

SUPERNATURAL POWER. WE COMMIT

OURSELVES TO BE FAITHFUL TO YOU AS SOVEREIGN

OF OUR LAND AND AS OUR PERSONAL

LORD AND SAVIOR. AMEN.

—LLOYD OGILVIE
Chaplain of the U.S. Senate, 1995–2003

THERE IS A VITAL INTERRELATIONSHIP BETWEEN OUR

PRAYERS AND AMERICA'S FUTURE GREATNESS.

GOD WANTS TO BLESS OUR LAND

THROUGH THE CHANNELS OF OUR PRAYER.

AMERICA'S MORAL GOODNESS AND SPIRITUAL

GREATNESS AND OUR SUCCESS

AND PROSPERITY ARE INSEPARABLE.

—LLOYD OGILVIE
U. S. Senate Chaplain, 1995–2003
& Honorary Committee Member
of *The Presidential Prayer Team*

THE ONLY SURE THING
WE CAN CLING TO

★ ★ ★

We are privileged to live in a country originally founded with a strong faith in God. From the very beginning, America has stood as a beacon of faith and freedom. The opening sentences of two of our country's most important documents—the Declaration of Independence and the Constitution—reaffirm belief in a Creator and His blessings of life, liberty, and the pursuit of happiness.

One aspect of the godly heritage bestowed upon us is prayer. Not only does this vital source direct and guide us, it also connects us intimately with our Father in heaven.

The world events of the past few years have driven many more Americans to their knees. Two years ago, who could imagine living under a color-coded system to indicate the threat of terrorist action on our own soil? Or that phrases like "weapons of mass destruction" would become part of the common vernacular? Faith is the only sure thing we can cling to in a world where fear bubbles just below the surface and nothing seems sure or safe.

Praying for the President and our nation's leaders during times like these is the best way we can continue to carry on the legacy of the believers who have come before us. Prayer is a mighty tool we can use to bless our leaders with guidance and wisdom. God can and will give our leaders wisdom if we ask Him. He will provide His protection for them.

And most importantly, He will give all of us His peace—peace that passes all understanding—even when the world around us is shaken by fear.

DAVID M. BROWNE
Family Christian Stores
President/CEO
& Honorary Committee Member
of *The Presidential Prayer Team*

OUR NATION WILL ONLY BE STRONGER

IF MORE OF US ARE ON OUR KNEES DAILY SEEKING

GOD'S WILL, WISDOM, AND FAVOR, AND

PRAYING IT BE SHOWERED UPON OUR LEADERS.

—DAVID M. BROWNE

A FAITH SET IN STONE

★ ★ ★

THE SUPREME COURT BUILDING

Did past governmental leaders value biblical principles as a basis for our government? Consider the witness of the Supreme Court Building, completed in 1932. As the Justices and others enter through the eastern portal of the Supreme Court Building, they pass beneath a huge relief sculpture. The three central figures represent the great lawgivers throughout history. The focal point of that sculpture is the figure of Moses, holding the Ten Commandments. Hermon MacNeil, the architect chosen for this portal, valued God's Word as given in the Decalogue so highly that he placed it on the building. The Supreme Court Building is yet another example of our nation's godly heritage.

IN NO OTHER WAY CAN THIS REPUBLIC BECOME

A WORLD POWER IN THE NOBLEST SENSE

OF THE WORD THAN BY PUTTING INTO HER LIFE

AND THE LIVES OF HER CITIZENS

THE SPIRIT AND PRINCIPLES OF THE GREAT

FOUNDER OF CHRISTIANITY.

—DAVID J. BREWER
Associate Justice
of the U. S. Supreme Court, 1889-1910

THE LIBERTY BELL

In 1751, the Pennsylvania State Assembly called for the forging of a bell to commemorate William Penn's original charter of the state. They included instructions requiring that a scripture verse be included on the bell. The verse is Leviticus 25:10, "Proclaim Liberty throughout all the land unto all the inhabitants thereof." Our founding fathers considered it important for all generations to know that God is the source of true freedom. On July 8, 1776, the Liberty Bell rang from the tower of Independence Hall in Philadelphia, calling citizens to the first public reading of the Declaration of Independence.

The magnificent monument to George Washington dominates the National Mall in Washington, D. C. As it towers over the other landmarks of our nation's capital, it proudly proclaims the profound impact he had on the founding of our nation. Even the cap of the monument includes the phrase "Praise be to God." When the cornerstone was laid on July 4, 1848, many citizens and dignitaries were present for the ceremony. President James K. Polk led the ceremony along with Speaker of the House, Robert C. Winthrop. Winthrop spoke eloquently about President Washington's life and impact, referring to his "exalted goodness and greatness to the influence of the Christian religion." After Winthrop's address, Rev. J. McJilton prayed a stirring and eloquent prayer:

And now, O Lord of all power and majesty, we humbly beseech Thee to let the wing of Thy protection be ever outspread over the land of Washington! May his people be Thy people! May his God be their God! Never from beneath the strong arm of Thy providence may they be removed; but, like their honored chief, may they acknowledge Thee in peace and in war, and ever serve Thee with a willing, faithful acceptable service! Hear our prayer, we beseech Thee, that the glory of this nation may never be obscured in the gloom of guilt; that its beauty may never be so marred by the foul impress of sin that the light of its religious character shall be dimmed. Open the eyes of the people, and let them see that it is their true interest to study Thy laws, to seek Thy favor, and to worship Thee with a faithful worship. . . . All these mercies and blessings we ask in the name and mediation of Jesus Christ, our most blessed Lord and Savior. Amen.

ARE WE ON GOD'S SIDE?

★ ★ ★

The Presidential Prayer Team is one of the major influences that has inspired me to fast and pray for forty days every year for the President, the nation, and the state of the world. Although it would be difficult to verify God's response to such prayers, there are prayers in the past for and by other presidents that have had a tremendous impact.

President Abraham Lincoln, whose spiritual life Susan Wales and I considered in our book *FAITH IN GOD AND GENERALS,* wrestled mightily with his faith during the dark hours of the Civil War. In the process, he had a clear call and came to know Jesus as his Lord and Savior. He recognized that he had been asking the wrong question, that is "whether God was on his side", and he began asking the right question, which is "Was he on God's side?"

Lincoln's death on Good Friday shook the nation, in part because it seemed to symbolize the atonement that was necessary for the years of bondage that the nation had imposed on African Americans. Although it took many years thereafter, the vestiges of that bondage were removed, and President Lincoln's words instruct us today to ask when we pray not whether God is on our side, but whether we are on His side.

DR. TED BAEHR
Chairman & CEO
Christian Film & Television Commission
& Honorary Committee Member
of *The Presidential Prayer Team*

WHEN I LEFT SPRINGFIELD, I ASKED
PEOPLE TO PRAY FOR ME; I WAS NOT A CHRISTIAN.
WHEN I BURIED MY SON—THE SEVEREST TRIAL
OF MY LIFE—I WAS NOT A CHRISTIAN.
BUT WHEN I WENT TO GETTYSBURG,
AND SAW THE GRAVES OF THOUSANDS OF OUR
SOLDIERS, I THEN AND THERE
CONSECRATED MYSELF TO CHRIST.

—PRESIDENT ABRAHAM LINCOLN

OUR NATION'S GODLY HERITAGE

A FAITH SET IN STONE:
THE LINCOLN MEMORIAL

★ ★ ★

*P*resident Abraham Lincoln is revered as a good man who was forged into a truly great, godly man during the fires of the Civil War. His second inaugural address is etched into one wall of the Lincoln Memorial, and the Gettysburg Address is carved into another. Those words have testified of Lincoln's faith to millions of visitors from around the world.

A Portion of Lincoln's Second Inaugural Address, March 4, 1865

Neither party expected for the war the magnitude or the duration which it has already attained. Neither anticipated that the cause of the conflict might cease with or even before the conflict itself should cease. Each looked for an easier triumph, and a result less fundamental and astounding. Both read the same Bible and pray to the same God, and each invokes His aid against the other. It may seem strange that any men should dare to ask a just God's assistance in wringing their bread from the sweat of other men's faces, but let us judge not, that we be not judged. The prayers of both could not be answered. That of neither has been answered fully. The Almighty has His own purposes. "Woe unto the world because of offenses; for it must needs be that offenses come, but woe to that man by whom the offense cometh." If we shall suppose that American slavery is one of those offenses which, in the providence of God, must needs come, but which, having continued through His appointed time, He now wills to remove, and that He gives to both North and South this terrible war as the woe due to those by whom the offense came, shall we discern therein any departure from those divine attributes which the believers in a living God always ascribe to Him?

Fondly do we hope, fervently do we pray, that this mighty scourge of war may speedily pass away. Yet, if God wills that it continue until all the wealth piled by the bondsman's two hundred and fifty years of unrequited toil shall be sunk, and until every drop of blood drawn with the lash shall be paid by another drawn with the sword, as was said three thousand years ago, so still it must be said "the judgments of the Lord are true and righteous altogether" (Psalm 19:9).

With malice toward none, with charity for all, with firmness in the right as God gives us to see the right, let us strive on to finish the work we are in, to bind up the nation's wounds, to care for him who shall have borne the battle and for his widow and his orphan, to do all which may achieve and cherish a just and lasting peace among ourselves and with all nations.

Fourscore and seven years ago our fathers brought forth on this continent a new nation, conceived in liberty and dedicated to the proposition that all men are created equal. Now we are engaged in a great civil war, testing whether that nation, or any nation so conceived and so dedicated, can long endure. We are met on a great battlefield of that war. We have come to dedicate a portion of that field as a final resting-place for those who here gave their lives that that nation might live. It is altogether fitting and proper that we should do this. But, in a larger sense, we cannot dedicate—we cannot consecrate—we cannot hallow—this ground. The brave men, living and dead, who struggled here have consecrated it, far above our poor power to add or detract. The world will little note, nor long remember what we say here, but it can never forget what they did here. It is for us the living, rather, to be dedicated here to the unfinished work which they who fought here have thus far so nobly advanced. It is rather for us to be here dedicated to the great task remaining before us—that from these honored dead we take increased devotion to that cause for which they gave the last full measure of devotion—that we here highly resolve that these dead shall not have died in vain—that this nation, under God, shall have a new birth of freedom and that government of the people, by the people, for the people, shall not perish from the earth.

IT IS OUR DUTY AND PRIVILEGE

TO UPHOLD OUR PRESIDENT IN PRAYER.

THE PRESIDENT NEEDS THE PRAYER AND WE NEED

THE DISCIPLINE OF PRAYING.

—DENNIS RAINEY

THE NATIONAL DAY OF PRAYER

(Annually on the first Thursday of May)

★ ★ ★

*S*ince the earliest moments of our nation's history, our leaders have called for national days of prayer, repentance and fasting. When the Continental Congress reached an impasse, Benjamin Franklin called for prayer with these words: "I have lived, Sir, a long time, and the longer I live, the more convincing proofs I see of this truth, that God governs in the affairs of men . . . And if a sparrow cannot fall to the ground without His notice, is it probable that an empire can rise without His aid? I therefore beg leave to move—that henceforth prayers imploring the assistance of Heaven, and its blessings on our deliberations, be held in this Assembly every morning before we proceed to business . . ."

Almost 100 years later, Abraham Lincoln called for national prayer in the midst of the Civil War. "WHEREAS, The Senate of the United States; devoutly recognizing the Supreme authority and just government of Almighty God in all the affairs of men and nations, has, by a resolution, requested the president to designate and set apart a day for National prayer and humiliation. And Whereas, it is the duty of nations, as well as of men, to owe their dependence upon the overruling power of God, to confess their sins and transgressions, in humble sorrow, yet with assured hope that genuine repentance will lead to mercy and pardon, and to recognize the sublime truth announced in the Holy

Scriptures and proven by all history, that those nations only are blessed whose God is the Lord."

Many other statesmen, presidents and leaders have called on the nation to turn to God in prayer. In 1952, President Truman signed a joint resolution of Congress, creating the National Day of Prayer, and in 1988 it became a law under the signature of President Ronald Reagan.

And in March 2003, resolutions in the House and Senate called for a day of humility, fasting, and prayer in response to the conflict in Iraq. Both resolutions acknowledged precedents from our nation's godly heritage and our people's reliance on God.

No matter how fervent our desires and requests, the Lord does not always respond the way we would choose. Sometimes His answers to our petitions are the very opposite of what we've sought—yet He always has our best interests in mind. When Jesus said, "Come to Me, all you who are weary and burdened, and I will give you rest," He added, "Take my yoke upon you and learn from Me" (Matthew 11:28-29). Coming to our Lord in acceptance and prayer requires us to also yield to His yoke. We must submit to where He leads and what He commands, even if He sends us in a direction we don't want to go.

—Shirley Dobson
Chairwoman, National Day of Prayer

SONGS OF GOD & COUNTRY

★ ★ ★

FAITH OF OUR FATHERS
(Frederick W. Faber, 1849)

Faith of our fathers, living still,
In spite of dungeon, fire and sword;
O how our hearts beat high with joy
Whenever we hear that glorious Word!

Faith of our fathers, holy faith!
We will be true to thee till death.

This hymn was sung at the funeral of President Franklin D. Roosevelt, held in the East Room of the White House in Washington, DC.

MY COUNTRY, 'TIS OF THEE
(Samuel F. Smith, 1832)

My country, 'tis of thee,
Sweet land of liberty,
Of thee I sing;
Land where my fathers died,
Land of the pilgrims' pride,
From every mountainside,
Let freedom ring!

Our fathers' God, to Thee,
Author of liberty,
To Thee we sing;
Long may our land be bright
With freedom's holy light;
Protect us by Thy might,
Great God, our King.

AMERICA THE BEAUTIFUL

(Katharine Lee Bates, 1913)

O beautiful for spacious skies,
For amber waves of grain,
For purple mountain majesties
Above the fruited plain.
America! America!
God shed His grace on thee,
And crown thy good with brotherhood
From sea to shining sea.

O beautiful for pilgrim feet
Whose stern impassioned stress.
A thoroughfare of freedom beat
Across the wilderness.
America! America!
God mend thine ev'ry flaw,
Confirm thy soul in self–control,
Thy liberty in law.

O beautiful for heroes proved
In liberating strife
Who more than self their country loved,
And mercy more than life.
America! America!
May God thy gold refine
Till all success be nobleness,
And every gain divine.

O beautiful for patriot dream
That sees beyond the years.
Thine alabaster cities gleam
Undimmed by human tears.
America! America!
God shed his grace on thee,
And crown thy good with brotherhood
From sea to shining sea.

GOD OF OUR FATHERS, WHOSE ALMIGHTY HAND

(Daniel C. Roberts, 1876)

God of our fathers, Whose almighty hand
Leads forth in beauty all the starry band
Of shining worlds in splendor through the skies
Our grateful songs before Thy throne arise.

Thy love divine hath led us in the past,
In this free land by Thee our lot is cast,
Be Thou our Ruler, Guardian, Guide and Stay,
Thy Word our law, Thy paths our chosen way.

From war's alarms, from deadly pestilence,
Be Thy strong arm our ever sure defense;
Thy true religion in our hearts increase,
Thy bounteous goodness nourish us in peace.

Refresh Thy people on their toilsome way,
Lead us from night to never ending day;
Fill all our lives with love and grace divine,
And glory, laud, and praise be ever Thine.

This is the official hymn of the United States Army. The U. S. Navy's hymn is "Eternal Father, Strong to Save."

THE EARTH IS THE LORD'S

AND ALL ITS FULLNESS,

THE WORLD AND

THOSE WHO DWELL THEREIN.

—PSALM 24:1

Providence has showered on this favored land blessings without number, and has chosen you as the guardians of freedom, to preserve it for the benefit of the human race. May He who holds in His hands the destinies of nations make you worthy of the favors He has bestowed and enable you, with pure hearts and pure hands and sleepless vigilance, to guard and defend to the end of time the great charge He has committed to your keeping.

—PRESIDENT ANDREW JACKSON,
IN HIS FAREWELL ADDRESS ON MARCH 4, 1837

I BELIEVE WITH ALL MY HEART

THAT STANDING UP FOR AMERICA MEANS

STANDING UP FOR THE GOD WHO HAS SO BLESSED

OUR LAND. WE NEED GOD'S HELP

TO GUIDE OUR NATION THROUGH STORMY SEAS.

BUT WE CAN'T EXPECT HIM TO PROTECT

AMERICA IN A CRISIS IF WE JUST LEAVE HIM

OVER ON THE SHELF IN OUR DAY-TO-DAY LIVING.

—PRESIDENT RONALD REAGAN

Chapter Two

★ ★ ★

PRAYING FOR OUR LEADERS AFFECTS MY HEART, HOME, NATION, & WORLD

I t sounds good. Pray for the President. Sure. No problem.

But does praying for the President really do any good? Absolutely!

As we bring our President and other leaders before the throne of God, we hold them more accountable to His holy will. We facilitate the Lord's work in their hearts. Then as our leaders draw closer to God, their decisions—affecting every facet of life in every community in our nation—become more and more in line with God's plan. Our schools are wiser, our defense is stronger, our streets are safer, and our neighbors here and around the world have better access to the goods and services they need.

But praying for our leaders also hits us personally. Praying about anything makes us better citizens of heaven by making our hearts more obedient and trusting in the Lord. Praying specifically for our leaders makes us better citizens of the United States by focusing our minds on the concerns of our nation. Prayer helps us pay closer attention to the needs of our neighbors and the leaders appointed to address those needs. When we pray for our leaders, we anticipate their righteousness more than we commiserate on their failings, we're more likely to see the Lord work in their lives.

From the White House to our houses, everybody wins when we pray for our leaders.

As a pastor I was blessed to have prayer partners, men and women whose powerful and protective prayers were responsible for any success that I knew as a husband, father and church leader during that time. Just as I felt the impact of their prayers on my life, I am sure that President Bush will be impacted by our prayers now. Prayer is powerful! And through prayer, God greatly multiplies our efforts. C. H. Spurgeon said, "Whenever God determines to do a great work, He first sets His people to pray." What we can do on our own is limited, but what God can do is endless. Please join me in praying for our President.

—JOHN C. MAXWELL
Founder, The INJOY Group
Honorary Committee Member
of *The Presidential Prayer Team*

PRAYER IS A MANDATE,
NOT AN OPTION

★ ★ ★

The first time I read in the Bible that we are supposed to pray "for kings and all who are in authority that we may live a quiet and peaceable life," I knew that praying for the President of the United States was not an option, it is a mandate (1 Timothy 2:2). That's why I try to pray for the President every day. First of all I ask God to put His hand of protection upon him and keep him out of harm's way. I pray that no weapon formed against him will prosper. I pray that he will have strength and good health so he will not grow weary. I, of course, pray the same for his family members too.

I also ask God to give the President wisdom, discernment, and knowledge for every decision he must make. I ask that he would find favor with the people of our nation and with other world leaders as well. Because the Bible says that the king's heart is in God's hand and like a river of water He turns it wherever He wants, I pray that the Lord would keep the President's heart turned toward Him at all times (Proverbs 21:1). That way, in the midst of the many voices he must listen to each day, he will be able to hear God's voice far above them all, guiding him in every situation.

When I pray this way, along with other specific concerns relative to what is happening in the nation on that day, it makes me feel more secure. It gives me that peace the Bible promises. And it helps to know that I am not the only one praying. Countless other people all over our nation are praying about the same issues. We may not all be in the same room or all praying at exactly the same time, but we are still praying together. And I believe God hears our prayers and will answer. This confidence helps me to sleep better at night.

STORMIE OMARTIAN
Author
& Honorary Committee Member
of *The Presidential Prayer Team*

Now more than ever we must heed God's call to pray for our President and our nation. It is not an option, it is a mandate. What a privilege to unite with others in fervent and powerful faith–filled prayers regarding the safety of our President and his family and the critical issues that face him daily. There is too much at stake not to do so.

—STORMIE OMARTIAN

PRAYING FOR THE PRESIDENT
HITS HOME

★ ★ ★

*P*raying for the President has deeply affected me! Obedience always does! God never makes "suggestions," but always COMMANDS. In 2 Timothy 2:1-2, Paul exhorted young Timothy: "I exhort . . . that supplications, prayers, intercessions . . . be made . . . for . . . all who are in authority . . . this is good and acceptable in the sight of God." As I have faithfully sought to be obedient, God has led me to other Scriptures that have added to my earnestness in prayer for the President: "The authorities that exist are appointed by God. Therefore whoever resists the authority resists the ordinance of God, and those who resist will bring judgment on themselves . . . for he is God's minister to you for good . . . for he is God's minister, an avenger to execute wrath on him who practices evil" (Romans 13:1-4).

To obey God, therefore, affects me in many ways:

• My obedience always pleases God.

• I then experience the Holy Spirit guiding me into intercessions I know nothing about. This always enriches my life, as I adjust my life to Scriptures given to me by the Holy Spirit.

• My family is always affected as they see me in prayer. They, too, pray!

• My intercession always affects the Kingdom of God, and God lets me have the joy of knowing this.

• God looks at my "little" in prayer and grants me "more" privileges to intercede. I have found myself speaking to United Nations ambassadors, government leaders, and other officials. I believe this grows out of faithful intercession for the President, as commanded by God.

What a privilege it has been, and still is, to pray for the President! My life will never be the same because of it.

HENRY BLACKABY
President, Henry Blackaby Ministries
& Honorary Committee Member
of *The Presidential Prayer Team*

From everyone who has been given much,
much will be demanded; and from the one who has been entrusted
with much, much more will be asked.

—Luke 12:48 (NIV)

ACT AS A FREE MAN, AND DO NOT

USE YOUR FREEDOM AS A COVERING FOR EVIL,

BUT USE IT AS BONDSLAVES OF GOD.

—1 Peter 3:16 (NAS)

ONLY A VIRTUOUS PEOPLE ARE CAPABLE

OF FREEDOM. AS NATIONS BECOME CORRUPT AND

VICIOUS, THEY HAVE MORE NEED OF MASTERS.

—BENJAMIN FRANKLIN

WE SHARE THEIR STORIES

★ ★ ★

How many presidential biographies have you seen on the New Releases shelves in your bookstore recently? No doubt there have been dozens. Each year historians, journalists, and biographers generate new books on America's past and present leaders. Books on men as diverse as John Adams, Theodore Roosevelt, John F. Kennedy, Ronald Reagan, and even our current president, George W. Bush, have all been bestsellers, and you can be sure that more are on the way.

Why is this? Why do Americans have an apparently insatiable appetite for stories about our leaders?

Because we know that the lives of American presidents are the lives of Americans. Their past is our shared past. The work they did, the decisions they made, the environment they created around themselves, the people they raised to follow them had massive effects on the course of American history. We seek to know about them because it helps us to know about ourselves.

Our lives can be dramatically affected by our president. We can feel almost immediately the weight of their policies on taxes, education, the environment, national defense, and other issues. In addition to those more tangible issues, the President in contemporary America has a great deal to do with the public mood. He is the international face of America to the world, and he is our symbol of where we stand as a country. Whether we recognize it or not, the President of the United States of America has a great deal to do with the everyday lives of Americans.

All this should motivate us to pray. God is sovereign, which does not mean that He dictates everything that happens in the world, but it does mean that He intercedes in and works through current events. We should pray that God will work through our President. That He will encourage him. That He will bless him with good counsel and wisdom. That the Holy Spirit will guide his choices, and the peace of God will guard his heart and mind in Jesus' name. We should pray that the President will be protected, that he will have rest, and that God's kingdom will come through his life and work.

LET'S DO IT. LET'S PRAY FOR OUR PRESIDENT.

LET'S BLESS HIM IN JESUS' NAME. AND ONE DAY,

PERHAPS NOT TOO LONG FROM NOW,

WE WILL BE READING BOOKS DESCRIBING

HOW AMERICA PROSPERED DURING HIS PRESIDENCY.

—TED HAGGARD
Senior Pastor, New Life Church
Colorado Springs, Colorado
& President, National
Association of Evangelicals
& Honorary Committee Member
of *The Presidential Prayer Team*

DEDICATING A PRESIDENTIAL
INAUGURATION TO ALMIGHTY GOD

★ ★ ★

*M*y father has had the honor of praying for or partici- pating in some way at eight presidential inaugurations, beginning with the ceremony for Lyndon Johnson in 1965. Now, as the inauguration of the forty-third President approached, the inaugural committee eagerly wanted Billy Graham to participate in the ceremo- ny. However, with weather forecasters predicting a cold, wet January morning in the Washington, D.C. area, my father's doctors had urged him not to put himself at risk by attending the inauguration, as it would be held outdoors. The Inaugural Committee, on behalf of President-elect Bush, called and asked me to give the invocation in my father's place.

With a deep sense of responsibility, I accepted the invitation and began to prepare. What an opportunity—to pray for the new President and his administration, as well as stand in for the man I love and respect so much.

I labored to construct a prayer that would invoke God's power. Millions would be listening. My deep desire was to focus the nation on Almighty God, ask for His blessing upon the incoming President and outgoing administration, and to bring glory to His Name.

Speaking into the bitter January air, I offered this prayer to God Almighty as my breath turned to white puffs:

Blessed are You, O Lord, our God.
Yours, O Lord, is the greatness and the power

And the glory and the majesty and the splendor;
For everything in heaven and earth is Yours.
Yours, O Lord, is the kingdom;
You are exalted as head over all.
Wealth and honor come from You;
You are the ruler of all things.
In Your hands are strength and power to exalt
And give strength to all.

I wanted to make clear at the very outset that as great a nation as America is, we are still dependent totally on the mercy of a holy and great God.

As President Lincoln once said,
We have been the recipients of the choicest bounties of heaven.
We have been preserved these many years in peace and prosperity.
We have grown in numbers, wealth, and power,
As no other nation has ever grown.
But we have forgotten God.
It behooves us, then, to humble ourselves before the Offended Power,
To confess our national sins,
And to pray for clemency and forgiveness.

I thought what Lincoln—one of our greatest presidents—had said was perfect for our present hour, in light of the previous eight years. Although in the same time period our country had experiences abundant prosperity, it was important to remember from where all blessings come—the mercy of our heavenly Father.

O Lord,
As we come together on this historic
And solemn occasion to inaugurate once again
A President and Vice President,
Teach us afresh that power, wisdom, and salvation
Come only from Your hand.

We pray, O Lord, for
President-elect George W. Bush
And Vice President-elect Richard B. Cheney,
To whom You have entrusted leadership
Of this nation at this moment in history.

We pray that You will help them bring our country together,
So that we may rise above partisan politics
And seek the larger vision of Your will for our nation.
Use them to bring reconciliation between the races
And healing to political wounds,
That we may truly become "one nation under God."

Our country had had a difficult and potentially divisive presidential election. Many citizens were bitter and disillusioned by the process and the outcome. There were more angry demonstrators protesting on the streets of Washington, D.C., than at any inauguration since the Vietnam War. We needed supernatural help to forgive one another, to heal wounds, to move on as a united people.

Give our new President and all who advise him
Calmness in the Face of Storms,
Encouragement in the Face of Frustration, and
Humility in the Face of Success.

Of course none of us could have realized, when I asked the Lord to give George W. Bush "calmness in the face of storms," just how great a storm would howl eight months later on September 11.

Give them the wisdom to know, and to do, what is right,
And the courage to say "No" to all that is contrary
to Your statutes and holy law.
Lord, we pray for their families
And especially for their wives,
Laura Bush and Lynne Cheney,
That they may sense Your Presence
And know Your Live.

Today we entrust to You
President and Senator Clinton,
And Vice President and Mrs. Gore.
Lead them as they journey through new doors of opportunity to serve others.

Now, O Lord, we dedicate this
Presidential Inaugural Ceremony to You.
May this be the beginning of a new down for America
As we humble ourselves before You
And Acknowledge You alone
As our Lord, our Savior, and our Redeemer.

Believing God was directing every word of my prayer, I had carefully chosen the word "Redeemer." Naturally, I was referring to the One who came to give His life for all who will ever draw breath on this planet. The redemption He purchased with the sacrifice of His own blood is available to anyone who will simply accept it—regardless of creed, nationality, religion, race, reputation, or personal history. I knew stating that there is no other Name by which an individual can be saved would grate on some ears and prick certain hearts. However, as a minister of the Gospel, I was not there to stroke the egos of men. My role was to acknowledge the all-powerful One and please Him. The Bible says: "Therefore, whoever confesses Me before men, him I will also confess before My Father who is in heaven."

We pray this in the Name of the Father,
And of the Son, the Lord Jesus Christ,
And of the Holy Spirit. Amen.

To my surprise, I heard amens and applause from an audience assembled primarily for political interests—not religious. I was gratified that those listening had understood the importance of seeking God's favor.

And seeking that favor in Jesus' Name, the only ground on which a sinner like me can come before a God who is so holy.

—FRANKLIN GRAHAM
President & CEO, Billy Graham Evangelistic Association
President, Samaritan's Purse
& Honorary Committee Co-chairman
of *The Presidential Prayer Team*

AMERICANS ARE A FREE PEOPLE, WHO KNOW
THAT FREEDOM IS THE RIGHT OF EVERY PERSON AND
THE FUTURE OF EVERY NATION. THE LIBERTY
WE PRIZE IS NOT AMERICA'S GIFT TO THE WORLD,
IT IS GOD'S GIFT TO HUMANITY. WE AMERICANS HAVE
FAITH IN OURSELVES, BUT NOT IN OURSELVES
ALONE. WE DO NOT KNOW—WE DO NOT CLAIM TO
KNOW—ALL THE WAYS OF PROVIDENCE,
YET WE CAN TRUST IN THEM, PLACING OUR
CONFIDENCE IN THE LOVING GOD BEHIND ALL OF
LIFE, AND ALL OF HISTORY. MAY HE GUIDE
US NOW. AND MAY GOD CONTINUE TO BLESS
THE UNITED STATES OF AMERICA.

—PRESIDENT GEORGE W. BUSH
State of the Union, Jan. 28, 2003

BE READY FOR GOD'S EXTRAORDINARY MOMENT

★ ★ ★

When I told Todd's story on national network television news shows on September 18, 2001, I hoped many people not only would realize what had happened aboard Flight 93, but also would understand the person Todd was. But I never could have guessed the impact of the story on all of America—or the world.

The chief of staff in the office of Representative J. C. Watts from Oklahoma called and invited me to attend the President's address to the nation in Washington, D.C., the evening of Thursday, September 20. It was time to head for the House Chamber to hear President Bush's speech. The aide led Chivon, Doug, and me through the hallways of the Capitol and up to the door. Just before we entered the Chamber, the aide said to me, "When the President addresses you, you can stand up and acknowledge him; you can wave, curtsy, bow, or whatever feels comfortable to you."

I was completely unprepared for the fact that the President even knew who I was, let alone that he would include me in his speech. *You've gotten me this far, God,* I thought. *I'll trust You for this, too.* That stopped the butterflies in my stomach as I entered the Chamber.

Although I was still very much mired in my own sense of devastation, it was nonetheless awe–inspiring when the room was called to order and the sergeant at arms called out, "Ladies and gentlemen, the President of the United States."

President Bush made his introductions and launched into his speech. I settled back as best I could and focused on listening to what the President had to say. This was an important speech for our nation; it would set the tone for our response to the terrorist attacks that had taken more than 3,000 lives, including the man I loved, the father of my children. I wanted to hear what the President planned for us to do.

"In the normal course of events, presidents come to this chamber to report on the state of the union," President Bush began. "Tonight, no such report is needed. It has already been delivered by the American people. We have seen it in the courage of passengers who rushed terrorists to save others on the ground. Passengers like an exceptional man named Todd Beamer. And would you please help me to welcome his wife, Lisa Beamer, here tonight?"

The room erupted in applause. It was the most humbling experience of my life to know that they were applauding me in an indirect effort to express their appreciation to Todd and the other heroes aboard Flight 93.

I had agreed earlier in the day to be a guest on CNN's *Larry King Live* after the speech. "How are you holding up?" Larry asked. "I know there's a part of this with all the attention and the heroics involved, but you said that it was your faith that (gets) you through, right?"

I just opened my mouth and said, "That's right. I know that Todd's death was not in vain. I see evidence of it all over as people have come up to me saying what an inspiration his faith and my faith have been to them. I just hope that it leads to a revival of faith in this country and the world. It's clear that that's what we need right now. It is time for that in our country."

LISA BEAMER
Widow of 9–11 hero Todd Beamer
& Honorary Committee Member
of *The Presidential Prayer Team*

THE PRICE OF FREEDOM

★ ★ ★

I'm convinced that one of the greatest things we can do for this nation is to pray. God calls on us to pray for our leaders, and we must. I love this country. And every day I thank God for the privilege of being born an American.

When you see the American flag, I hope you're reminded, not just of what it stands for, but what it cost. We owe a debt to the heroic men and women who have died to ensure that we have the freedoms we enjoy and too often take for granted. When we fail to pray, we are not doing our part to ensure their sacrifices were not in vain. We owe it to God and to our country to pray for the United States of America.

We've seen it flying torn and tattered
We've seen her stand the test of time
And through it all the fools have fallen
There she stands

By the dawn's
Early light
And through the fight
She stands

—From "There She Stands"
by Michael W. Smith & Wes King

Truly in this time, for this generation, the call to prayer could not be more important. The young people of our nation are becoming involved in worship and prayer in a way they never have before. Now is the time to summon all of our energies for this important effort of prayer—so God's purposes may be served and His will may be done. I've been fortunate to spend time with several presidents personally, and my respect for these men is tremendous, because they have helped preserve the freedoms we enjoy. I urge you to continue to pray for the President and his advisors regarding the tough decisions that they will have to make in the coming weeks and months. The Presidential Prayer Team is one way we can help leave a legacy of freedom to our children. May the Lord continue to draw us all closer to Him in awesome ways, and as we seek Him, may God truly bless America.

—MICHAEL W. SMITH
Christian Recording Artist
& Honorary Committee Co-chairman
of *The Presidential Prayer Team*

THE IMPACT OF PRAYER

ON OUR KNEES, STANDING STRONG

★ ★ ★

"Never has there been a time in the history of the world that prayer and the need to seek God on a daily basis has been any more vital. The United States has been home to me since I came over with my family from my homeland of Australia as a teenager.

I have so appreciated the American spirit on which the nation was established—with founding fathers that allowed God to be openly worshipped. I join concerned believers in standing together to preserve those liberties.

I also heartily support *The Presidential Prayer Team* in encouraging America to pray. I challenge my generation to stand and make a difference in the world around us. Be encouraged and stand strong for Jesus!

REBECCA ST. JAMES
Christian Recording Artist
& Honorary Committee Member
of *The Presidential Prayer Team*

I believe in the power of prayer.
I have seen miracles happen when God's people have prayed.
That's why I want to encourage young and old alike
to pray for our president, that God will use
this man to help turn this nation back to Him.

—REBECCA ST. JAMES

HAVE I NOT COMMANDED YOU?

BE STRONG AND OF GOOD COURAGE;

DO NOT BE AFRAID, NOR BE

DISMAYED, FOR THE LORD YOUR GOD IS

WITH YOU WHEREVER YOU GO.

—JOSHUA 1:9

This is our time to be strong
This is our time to rise up…
To stand and be counted!
This is our time to believe
To know in our God we are free
Let the world know to Him we belong.

—FROM "STAND"

BY REBECCA ST. JAMES & REGGIE HAMM

OBEYING GOD—
OUR ULTIMATE LEADER

★ ★ ★

*O*ur President is in an awesome position of responsibility. As the leader of God's most powerful democracy in the world, it is critical that believers lift him up before God in prayer. It is our Christian mandate to intercede on behalf of our leader, our nation, and our world.

God has called each of us to stand in the gap and we have an ongoing responsibility to pray, seek His face, humble ourselves and turn away from sin. God cannot lie. He will heal the land. The United States of America is in need of healing today more than ever before.

BISHOP GEORGE D. MCKINNEY
Pastor and Founder, St. Stephen's Church of God in Christ Ministries
& Honorary Committee Member of *The Presidential Prayer Team*

THEREFORE I EXHORT FIRST OF ALL THAT
SUPPLICATIONS, PRAYERS, INTERCESSIONS AND
GIVING OF THANKS BE MADE FOR ALL MEN, FOR
KINGS AND ALL WHO ARE IN AUTHORITY, THAT WE
MAY LEAD A QUIET AND PEACEABLE LIFE IN ALL
GODLINESS AND REVERENCE. FOR THIS IS GOOD AND
ACCEPTABLE IN THE SIGHT OF GOD OUR SAVIOR

— 1 TIMOTHY 2:1–4

THE KING'S HEART IN THE LORD'S HAND

★ ★ ★

God is clear about the way things work in national leadership.

One of the greatest leaders in history, Solomon, said "The king's heart is in the hand of the Lord" (Proverbs 21:1). That means, in spite of what we may think about the power of the office, the real power of the office is under God's direction. Didn't Jesus tell Pilate he would have no power at all if it weren't given to him by the Father? So in a very real sense, Jesus is the King of kings, the President of presidents, Governor of governors.

If we want to move the heart of the king, we do it by moving the hand of God. And we know from God's word that we move the hand of God through the mysterious power of prayer.

How can we best influence our nation? How can we effectively support our national leaders? It's by praying for God to work, move and direct our President and national leaders. Knowing that the heart of the President is in the hand of God, we can go directly to the King of kings knowing He will direct the course of the nations.

WAYNE PEDERSON
President and Chief Operating Officer,
Mission America Coalition
& Honorary Committee Member
of *The Presidential Prayer Team*

For years, Christians have desired an opportunity to partner with the White House in support of godly principles and faith in God. Now the doors for prayer partnership are wide open for believers to support our leadership and encourage godly participation.

—WAYNE PEDERSON

NO PEOPLE OUGHT TO FEEL GREATER OBLIGATIONS

TO CELEBRATE THE GOODNESS OF

THE GREAT DISPOSER OF EVENTS AND THE DESTINY

OF NATIONS THAN THE PEOPLE OF THE

UNITED STATES...AND TO THE SAME DIVINE AUTHOR

OF EVERY GOOD AND PERFECT GIFT

WE ARE INDEBTED FOR ALL THOSE PRIVILEGES AND

ADVANTAGES, RELIGIOUS AS WELL AS

CIVIL, WHICH ARE SO

RICHLY ENJOYED IN THIS FAVORED LAND.

—PRESIDENT JAMES MADISON

PRAYER CHANGES LIVES AND HISTORY.

PRAYING FOR AMERICA'S OFFICIALS WILL EMPOWER

THEM TO PROVIDE INSPIRED, COURAGEOUS

MORAL LEADERSHIP DURING

THE DOMESTIC AND INTERNATIONAL

CRISES FACING ALL AMERICANS.

—GENERAL JOHN A. WICKHAM
& Honorary Committee Member
of *The Presidential Prayer Team*

A CALL FOR NATIONAL REPENTANCE

★ ★ ★

"The prayer of a righteous man is powerful and effective" (James 5:16, NIV). The principle presented is that our obedience and our prayers are divinely linked. How we live out our lives, by either choosing to obey God's will or choosing to walk in the ways of the world, significantly impacts our relationship with our Heavenly Father and our prayer life. E. M. Bounds put it this way:

"If we want to have God in the prayer closet, God must have us out of the prayer closet. The prayer closet is not a confessional, simply, but the hour of Holy communion, of high and sweet communication, and of intense intercession."

God, through prayer, can shape our will, our character, and our heart's desires so we can live a life honoring to Him.

If our conduct is not in line with God's will, we must move to repentance. Psalm 66 tells us that if we cherish or harbor any unconfessed sin, it will put a wall between us and God that will inhibit our prayers. When we go into God's presence, a God who knows no sin, we must enter with a repentant heart. So part of our prayers should include repentance like David's when he stated in Psalm 139:

"Search me O God, and know my heart: test me and know my thoughts. Point out anything in me that offends you and lead me along the path of everlasting life."

A repentant heart is so important in approaching God that Jesus included our need to seek His forgiveness in the words of the Lord's Prayer; "...forgive us our sins..."

At a time in our nation's history when we seek God's divine blessing, we must first humble ourselves and seek His forgiveness. For as we look across our cultural landscape, we see:

- 41 million babies being killed since *Roe v. Wade* passed in 1973,
- corruption toppling corporate giants
- pornography being protected by our Constitution
- God being removed from the public as "Under God" is challenged in our Pledge of Allegiance.

God has made His will clear in 2 Chronicles 7:14 through a conditional promise:

If my people, who are called by my name, will humble themselves and pray and seek my face and turn from their wicked ways, then will I hear from Heaven and forgive their sin and heal their land.

We must do our part, so God will do His. As we pray for our President and this great nation, let's start by seeking His forgiveness and asking Him to stir in the hearts of His people a desire for righteousness so our prayers will be powerful and effective!

"Righteousness exalts a nation, but sin is a disgrace to any people" (Proverbs 14:34).

JAMES WEIDMANN
Vice Chairman, National Day of Prayer Task Force
& Honorary Committee Member
of *The Presidential Prayer Team*

GOD GIVES THE VICTORY

Alarmed, Jehoshaphat resolved to inquire of the LORD, and he proclaimed a fast for all Judah. The people of Judah came together to seek help from the LORD; indeed, they came from every town in Judah to seek him.

—2 CHRONICLES 20: 3–4   NIV

★ ★ ★

*I*f you haven't read the story of Jehoshaphat and the fight against the Moabites and Ammonites, take time to read the entire story and you will discover God's faithfulness for those who seek His help.

Jehoshaphat learned that the Moabites and the Ammonites were coming to make war against the people of Judah. Immediately, Jehoshaphat cried out to the Lord for help, and also encouraged the people of Judah to do so as well. Together, they cried out for deliverance, recalled the protection the Lord had provided His people in the past, and acknowledged their helplessness and God's ultimate power.

The Lord in return assured Jehoshaphat and the people of Judah that the battle was not theirs to fight, but the battle belonged to the Lord. God told the people to, "Take up your positions, stand firm, and see the deliverance the LORD will give you" (2 Chronicles 20:17, NIV).

And that they did. The people trusted the Lord and sent out their armies led by a group of men whose sole purpose was to continually lead the people in praising God. What type of a leader would do that? One who wants to have the praise singers be the first to die? A leader who wants the enemy to know they are coming by their singing? No. Judah's leader wanted it to be clear who was fighting the battle and who would give the people of Judah ultimate protection and victory—the Lord.

What was the result? Right before their eyes the Lord "set ambushes against the men of Ammon and Moab and Mount Seir who were invading Judah, and they were defeated. The men of Ammon and Moab rose up against the men from Mount Seir to destroy and annihilate them. After they finished slaughtering the men from Seir, they helped to destroy one another" (2 Chronicles 20:22–23, NIV).

God fought the battle for Judah and brought them ultimate victory. All Judah did was acknowledge the Lord and cry out to Him for help.

That is the type of leader I want in my country—one who sees trouble coming and not only cries to the Lord for protection, but encourages his people to do so as well. What is my responsibility? To cry out to God on behalf of my country and its people, and continually lift up the leaders of this country in prayer, asking the Lord to give them strength, wisdom, and a humble knee that bows before Him. Only then will we have victory together.

RON BLUE
Founder and Chairman, Ronald Blue & Company
& Honorary Committee Member
of *The Presidential Prayer Team*

IF GOD IS ALWAYS WITH US,

THEN HE CAN PRESERVE AND PROTECT US,

OUR COUNTRY, AND OUR WAY OF LIFE. PRAYING FOR

OUR LEADERS ENSURES THAT WE ARE PART OF THE

GRAND PLAN FOR OUR COUNTRY.

—RON BLUE

For we must consider that we shall be as a City upon a hill.
The eyes of all people are upon us. So that if we shall deal falsely with our
God in this task we have undertaken, and so cause
Him to withdraw His present help from us,
we shall be made a story and a byword throughout the world.

—JOHN WINTHROP
Governor of the Massachusetts Bay Colony, 1630

SPEECH WRITING

★ ★ ★

The other day I was reading an article in *TIME* magazine about Michael Gerson, the speechwriter for President George W. Bush. It described the intensity and scrutiny that goes into writing a speech for a President. When crafting an important speech, Michael Gerson goes to great pains in selecting the exact verbs, adverbs, nouns and adjectives. Every word is carefully scrutinized to fit in the overall strategy of the administration. No word is in a speech by accident. No noun or pronoun is used carelessly; rather, each fits perfectly.

Now if a President goes to such great lengths to handcraft every solitary word so that his message comes across clear and concise, then you know that God went to even greater lengths to make certain that every noun and verb, every adjective and preposition in every single solitary sentence in the Bible is handcrafted by the Holy Spirit, handpicked to fit into God's overall message for His people. There are no careless words in the Bible. There are no thoughtless phrases. Everything fits perfectly.

Take Philippians 3:20 for instance. It says, "And we eagerly await a Savior . . . " That word "eagerly" was put there for a purpose. God doesn't want us to merely wait; we're to wait eagerly. And look at Ephesians 1:3. It says that we have been blessed with every spiritual blessing in Christ. Not some blessings or a few blessings, but *every* possible benefit of Christ's work has been and is being applied to our lives.

I could go on, but I don't want to sound like, well . . . a speechwriter. The point is, if the President of the United States sweats over every word, then you know the Holy Spirit has taken far greater pains with the Word of God.

And friend, this is helpful to remember as we come before the Lord in prayer. First Peter 4:11 tells us that, "If anyone speaks, he should do it as one speaking the very words of God." We don't need a presidential speechwriter to remind us of the importance of preparing our hearts and minds before praying . . . of the importance of seeking God's heart before speaking . . . of searching for His overall strategy before petitioning . . . of weighing our words before offering them at the seat of God. After all, this isn't the Oval Office, this is the glorious throne of the Lord of the universe!

Your words have power before the Lord. More power than you realize. For Isaiah 55:11–12 assures, ". . . so is My word that goes out from My mouth: It will not return to Me empty, but will accomplish what I desire and achieve the purpose for which I sent it. You will go out in joy and be led forth in peace."

So surrender your soul . . . center your thoughts . . . ask the Spirit for help . . . weigh your words . . . then pray with joy and certainty that God will take those words and accomplish His grand and glorious purpose!

JONI EARECKSON TADA
Founder and President, Joni and Friends
& Honorary Committee Co-chairman
of *The Presidential Prayer Team*

BEFORE ALL ELSE, WE SEEK, UPON OUR

COMMON LABOR AS A NATION, THE BLESSINGS

OF ALMIGHTY GOD. AND THE HOPES IN

OUR HEARTS FASHION THE DEEPEST PRAYERS OF OUR

WHOLE PEOPLE. MAY WE PURSUE THE RIGHT—

WITHOUT SELF-RIGHTEOUSNESS.

MAY WE KNOW UNITY—WITHOUT CONFORMITY.

MAY WE GROW IN STRENGTH—WITHOUT

PRIDE IN SELF. MAY WE, IN OUR DEALINGS WITH ALL

PEOPLES OF THE EARTH, EVER SPEAK TRUTH

AND SERVE JUSTICE. AND SO SHALL AMERICA—

IN THE SIGHT OF ALL MEN OF GOOD WILL—

PROVE TRUE TO THE HONORABLE PURPOSES THAT

BIND AND RULE US AS A PEOPLE IN ALL THIS TIME

OF TRIAL THROUGH WHICH WE PASS.

—President Dwight D. Eisenhower
In his inaugural address, Jan. 21, 1957

Chapter Three

★ ★ ★

HOW & WHAT WE NEED TO PRAY

God doesn't need to hear our prayers in order to know what's going on with us and with our country. He's already actively involved. God is always listening to us, taking care of us, but in prayer we acknowledge Him as our ultimate leader. We remind Him—and ourselves—that He's in control and that no matter what happens, His eternal plan will prevail. Our prayers just keep our hearts and minds more in line with that plan.

So how do we pray effective, fervent prayers on behalf of the President and other leaders? How do we make Him listen? What kinds of prayers does God like to answer? How do we help our children understand and participate in prayers for our nation?

Following are several insights that address these and other prayer questions. Just open your spirit, open your Bible, and let the devotionals guide you into a more intimate prayer life, especially in your prayers for this country.

Let us pray.

ONE WAY TO PRAY
FOR THE PRESIDENT

★ ★ ★

D o you ever wonder just how you can pray for the President? Or do you sometimes find that your prayers for the President or other national leaders seem to be "dry" or simply repetitious?

I have found that one of the most meaningful ways to pray for the President is to use Scripture. For example, there is a significant portion of Scripture to use in praying that is shared near the end of the life of King David.

During the initial preparations for the building of the Temple, David shared some wonderful words of encouragement with His son Solomon. With just a slight modification, those words provide a significant prayer for us too use in praying for our President.

As I write these words, I do not know who will be serving as our President or what challenges he may be facing today when you pray this prayer. But I do believe that you can be used powerfully as you pray this prayer based upon I Chronicles 22:11–13:

"Dear Lord,

*I pray for the President of the United States and
for those leaders who serve with him. I pray that you will be with him
and that he will have success in all that he does. I pray that
you would give him discretion and understanding and that
he would be strong and courageous. May he not be afraid or become
discouraged. Instead, may he trust in you with all of his heart!
I pray this in the wonderful name of Jesus,
Amen*

DR. PAUL CEDAR
CEO and Chairman, Mission America Coalition
& Honorary Committee Member
of *The Presidential Prayer Team*

*Now, my son, may the LORD be with you;
and may you prosper, and build the house of the LORD your God,
as He has said to you. Only may the LORD give you wisdom
and understanding, and give you charge concerning Israel,
that you may keep the law of the LORD your God.
Then you will prosper, if you take care to fulfill the statutes
and judgments with which the LORD charged Moses concerning Israel.
Be strong and of good courage; do not fear nor be dismayed.*

—1 CHRONICLES 22:11-13

AS THE FAMILY GOES, SO GOES

THE NATION AND SO GOES THE WHOLE WORLD

IN WHICH WE LIVE.

—POPE JOHN PAUL II

*America was born a Christian nation. America was
born to exemplify that devotion to the elements of righteousness, which
are derived from the revelations of Holy Scriptures.
Part of the destiny of Americans lies in their daily perusal
of this great book of revelations. That if they would see America free
and pure they will make their own spirits
free and pure by this baptism of the Holy Spirit.*

—PRESIDENT WOODROW WILSON

FIVE SECRETS TO PRAYING PRAYERS OF FAITH

★ ★ ★

You want God to answer your prayers and you've already taken some steps to build your faith. Now it's time to pray. What is it about prayer that demands faith? What can you do while praying to bolster your faith? Here are five secrets I've learned about how to pray prayers of faith.

Begin with Reverence

Our God is an awesome God. "How awesome is the LORD Most High, the great King over all the earth!" (Psalm 47:2, NIV). He is a majestic God. "O LORD, our Lord, how majestic is your name in all the earth!" (Psalm 8:1, NIV). When you pray to Him, you ought to acknowledge His unmatchable character. That's why Jesus taught His disciples to to begin their prayers, "Our Father in heaven, hallowed be your name" (Matthew 6:9).

Pray the Promises

Another way to build your faith while praying is to pray the promises of God. Demonstrate to God that you take His Word seriously by quoting His promises to Him while you pray. Read the promises from God is His Word. Pray the promises to God in response.

Expand Your Faith

In his prophecy about God's future plans for Jerusalem, Isaiah borrowed a figure from the nomadic life of the bedouin: "Enlarge the place of your tent, stretch your tent curtains wide, do not hold back;

lengthen your cords, strengthen your stakes" (Isaiah 54:2, NIV). Like a nomad blessed of God with so many children that He had to enlarge His tent, God will one day bless Jerusalem in a way that will astound the world.

End with Anticipation

Someone mused, "Blessed is he who expecteth nothing, for he shall not be disappointed." When you pray, is your final "Amen" just a "hello" to doubt? Do you sign off with the sigh, "Well, that probably didn't get me anywhere?" Or do you end your prayers in anticipation of an answer?

DR. WOODROW KROLL
President, Back to the Bible
& Honorary Committee Member
of *The Presidential Prayer Team*

I HAVE ALWAYS SAID THAT PRAYER WORKS

BEST WHEN NOTHING WORKS AT ALL. THERE ARE

DAYS WHEN THE PRESIDENT MUST THINK

NOTHING IS WORKING. THOSE ARE THE DAYS

HE ESPECIALLY NEEDS OUR PRAYERS.

—WOODROW KROLL

IF WE ASK, GOD WILL ANSWER

*"Call to Me and I will answer you, and show you great
and mighty things which you do not know."*

—JEREMIAH 33:3

Today, we are faced with many stressful situations and decisions that affect our country and in turn affects us personally. The Bible states clearly that God wants us to come to Him in prayer, to share our innermost thoughts, fears and hopes for a bright and peaceful tomorrow. He has promised that if we call to Him, He will answer and when we trust Him, He will show us great and mighty things, which only God knows.

Sometimes, I believe we miss the mark in life because we cannot see beyond our own little circle. God has poured out on this country great power, wealth, and other blessings. Therefore, as it says in Philippians 4:6–7, we should, *"Be anxious for nothing, but in everything by prayer and supplication, with thanksgiving, let your request be made known to God; and the peace of God, which surpasses all understanding will guard your hearts and minds, through Jesus Christ."*

What a wonderful opportunity we have as Christians to praise the Lord and call upon His divine protection for the leaders of this country and all who help guide this nation through war and peace. Let us go to our knees everyday and call upon the Lord; He is ready, willing and able.

JACK COUNTRYMAN
Publisher, J. Countryman Gift Books
& Honorary Committee Member of *The Presidential Prayer Team*

TO PRAY FOR OUR PRESIDENT IS A PRIVILEGE

THAT WE AS CHRISTIANS SHOULD ENDORSE AND

MAKE A PART OF OUR DAILY LIVES.

THE WISDOM OF GOD TO DIRECT THE ACTIVITIES

OF THIS COUNTRY IS THE ONLY ANSWER

FOR OUR FUTURE. MAY GOD GIVE

OUR PRESIDENT WISDOM AND STRENGTH.

—JACK COUNTRYMAN

PRAY FOR HONEST & WISE LEADERS

"When the righteous are in authority, the people rejoice; but when a wicked man rules, the people groan . . . The king establishes the land by justice, but he who receives bribes overthrows it."

—PROVERBS 29:2, 4

★ ★ ★

Scripture tells us that righteous leadership leads to a joyful population, and that a just leader brings stability to the land. By contrast, a wicked ruler causes the people to groan and fosters instability in a nation.

As Christians we must care about and pray for the character of the current President of the United States, and for all future presidents. According to God's word, the President's personal pursuit of righteousness and justice will directly impact the happiness of Americans and the stability of our nation.

Temptations to unrighteousness will come to our presidents in a variety of ways. In addition to the temptations that are "common to man," a president will face unique temptations related to holding the most powerful position in the world.

We should pray that our presidents avoid using their office for personal gain, or to exact personal revenge against political opponents. We should pray they are surrounded by good and godly counselors who are seeking what's best for the nation.

Because of the amount of attention, ridicule and criticism presidents receive, we should pray for their humility and against outbursts of anger and self–righteousness.

Every president need only take a walk through the White House to the State Dining Room to remember the high character needed in that high office, a high character demonstrated by so many of our past presidents. In the State Dining Room, carved into the mantel below a portrait of Abraham Lincoln, is this inscription:

> *I pray Heaven to Bestow the Best of Blessings on THIS HOUSE and on All that shall hereafter Inhabit it. May none but honest and Wise Men ever rule under this roof.*

That prayer was offered by our second president, John Adams, on his second night in the White House. May it be our prayer as well.

LEN MUNSIL
President and General Counsel
The Center for Arizona Policy
& Honorary Committee Member
of *The Presidential Prayer Team*

THE BIRTH OF OUR NATION WAS BATHED IN CHRISTIAN PRAYER. NOW, AT THIS CRITICAL TIME IN OUR NATION'S HISTORY, WE ARE AGAIN REMINDED OF OUR PRESIDENT'S NEED FOR DAILY GUIDANCE AND DIRECTION FROM ALMIGHTY GOD.

—LEN MUNSIL

PRAYER IS A RADICAL CONVERSION

OF ALL OUR MENTAL PROCESSES BECAUSE IN PRAYER

WE MOVE AWAY FROM OURSELVES, OUR

WORRIES, PREOCCUPATION, AND

SELF–GRATIFICATION—AND DIRECT ALL

THAT WE RECOGNIZE AS OURS TO GOD IN THE

SIMPLE TRUST THAT THROUGH HIS LOVE,

ALL WILL BE MADE NEW.

—Henri Nouwen

Our strength lies in spiritual concepts.
It lies in public sensitiveness to evil. Our greatest danger is
not from invasion by foreign armies.
Our dangers are that we may commit suicide from
within by complaisance with evil,
or by public tolerance of scandalous behavior.

—PRESIDENT HERBERT HOOVER

PRAYING WITH CHILDREN

*Strong Families Use a Biblical Tool
to Pray for our President*

★ ★ ★

All throughout the Scriptures, you can see a powerful tool that the Lord used to make Himself known to those who love Him. That same tool is one we can use to help our children understand how to pray for our President and others. While this tool isn't given a specific name in Scripture, I call it an "emotional word picture." It's one of the primary methods Jesus used to help His disciples "get the picture" when He wanted to communicate something important to them. It's also a "visual aid" we can use to help our children understand what our President does and how to pray for him (or her).

To see this tool in Scripture, let's look first at a few of what are hundreds of examples. When Psalm 23 was written, David was reflecting on being hunted by those who sought his life. In that context, he wrote the familiar words that give a clear "picture" of a God of comfort in difficult times, "The Lord is my shepherd, I shall not want. He makes me to lie down in green pastures" (Psalm 23:1–2). On the night before He was crucified, Jesus told His disciples, "In My Father's house are many mansions; if it were not so, I would have told you. I go to prepare a place for you" (John 14:2). Whether it was a prophet, an Old Testament King or Jesus Himself, "word pictures" (often in the form of a parable) were used to "make tangible the intangible." We can't see the omnipotent, omniscient, eternal Father, but the Psalmist tells us that part of His character is reflected in the heart of a Shepherd. That's a picture we can understand and draw comfort from. And for Jesus, He helped calm the fears of His disciples by giving them a "word picture"

of a heavenly home that awaited each them—a place where He would be also.

And how exactly does that help us pray for the President?

Particularly with younger children, but for older children as well, praying for the President can be a very "intangible" prayer. It's difficult for an adult, much less a child, to get their hands around the tremendous domestic and international responsibilities that the elected leader of our country faces. So why not do what Scripture does and use a picture to "make tangible the intangible?"

For example, think about some of the responsibilities that make up the President's daily or weekly tasks and then link them with an object or story. Let's say you're at the dinner table when you pray for the President. Get a map and lay it out on the table. Pick two cities on the map and have your children find each one. Then have your kids pick a route, either using major highways or a "backwoods road" from one city to the other. Kids like "connecting the dots" and once each child has traced their own route, then share with them. "Did you know that one thing our President has to do every day in leading our country is like what we just did?" Then share with them that part of a President's responsibilities lies in deciding the direction our country needs to go—politically and to a large part economically, he has to decide the "road" we need to take as a country. Now take a moment to pray as a family for our President to have God's wisdom as he seeks to have the United States travel the best route from where we are to where we need to go in the future.

Do you get the picture? Your kids will when it comes to praying for our President—especially if you help them "make tangible the intangible" by using this biblical communication tool.

DR. JOHN TRENT
President of StrongFamilies.com
& Honorary Committee Member
of *The Presidential Prayer Team*

PRAYER IS OUR MOST POWERFUL WEAPON

FOR CHANGE, AND WE MUST USE IT TO PROTECT

OURSELVES EVERY MINUTE OF EVERY DAY.

—JOHN TESH
Musician, Radio Host
& Honorary Committee Member
of *The Presidential Prayer Team*

INTERCESSORY PRAYER HELPS BELIEVERS ACT WITH HOPE FOR OTHERS

A devotional based on "Somebody's Praying Me Through,"
performed by Allen Asbury

"It may be my Mother . . . it might be my Dad . . . or an old friend I forgot I had, but whoever it is I'm so glad that, 'Somebody's praying me through'."

★ ★ ★

The Christian tradition of intercessory prayer, exemplified vividly by Jesus in the Gospels, can be a compass that sets the way. That's the message of "Somebody's Praying Me Through," written by Darrell R. Brown and Ty Lacy and sung by Allen Asbury on his debut album.

"Everyone can relate to this song. Everyone has a story where someone else's prayers carried you through a painful time. Or maybe it's a story where you've prayed for someone you love who is hurting—where you fall on your knees because you don't know what else to do, so you pray and pray and pray," says Allen, an Honorary Committee member of *The Presidential Prayer Team*.

The Book of Psalms, a rich source for understanding the need for intercession, gives voice to humanity's cry in the darkness. For instance, in Psalm 13 King David petitions, "How long, O LORD? Will you forget me forever? How long will You hide Your face from me?" Passages like

Psalm 13 and also Psalm 88 acknowledge the unsettling experiences of even the faithful seeker of God.

Intercessory prayer is the Christian community's response to the cries of the individual believer. Although God hears when Christians cry out to Him in their own pain, intercessory prayer strengthens the Body by causing believers to walk together, holding each other's hands in this life. It is God's ordained way for responding to the pain of those around us and ultimately allows for greater glory and praise given to the Father. Intercessory prayer builds community in the Body of Christ. It reminds each of us of our need for fellow believers.

"In 'Somebody's Praying Me Through,' a key word for me is 'through.' Praying through the difficult times, your own or others," says Allen. "This is not a quick–fix to pain, it is a process, a state–of–mind during a trial. And though you might not get everything you asked for, you will receive what you hoped for, because He is the author of hope." Hope is a key word in the subject of prayer. During difficult times, hope is an extraordinary gift which is bestowed on believers by the Spirit in the lives of those who are praying, and those who are being prayed for. In our own weakness, we will not be able to sense new opportunities or even new ways to pray for someone else or for ourselves. The Spirit works through intercessory prayer to bring hope to the hopeless.

ACTING WITH HOPE

The Christian faith believes hope is available to all through the gift of prayer. Praying someone through, or being prayed through trouble, is an act of hope.

IF YOU ARE IN NEED OF HOPE:

1) *Ask for prayer*—Confide your need in people you trust. It doesn't matter if they are near or far, but you must be able to communicate with them. Personal conversation is best. The phone or e–mail will do. Regardless, being able to articulate your need removes your concern from the darkest corner of your mind and into a place where its mysterious burden on you begins to diminish.

2) *Go in prayer*—Praying for yourself is not selfish, usually, but rather an act of self–care. Breathing air into your lungs is not self–centered but necessary for survival. Prayer is like breath for the soul.

God, though, in His wisdom, knew not to require it of us. In our hurt and pain, we can blame God and not feel like talking to Him. That's OK. He can take it. But try—at least mutter something like David did: "How long, O Lord?" Our petitions are heard, and a time will come when that communication feels good again. All along the most reticent prayer can quench our thirsty soul with cool, clear drinks of hope.

3) *Hope and wait*—The end of one season births the beginning of another. The pain of what was held dear is no less difficult, maybe seemingly overwhelming, but the embryo of new start, new opportunity is developing. Hope takes time to grow and thrive.

Acting with hope means, also, praying for others. Intercessory prayer is a rebellious cry "No!" in the face of another's chaos. Praying for someone else is acting for them as a source of hope.

WHEN YOU HOPE FOR OTHERS:

1) *Have an active prayer life*—For some, stating this is preaching to the choir. For others, it's like changing the oil in the car: it's got to be done regularly or everything breaks down. Whatever your situation, pray today with God for the world around you, and continue to do so.

2) *Try keeping a list of people for whom you pray and a brief reminder of their need*—Naming names is not so much for God's sake as much as it is for our own. They remain on our lips and are therefore not forgotten.

3) *Remind yourself to pray.* Decide to pray for your friend or loved one every day for four minutes at 4:00, or every morning when you pass a road–sign on the way to work. Write yourself a note and place it on your bathroom mirror. Wear a special necklace or bracelet which will remind you of your loved one's need. In our busy lives, good intentions need the assistance of good reminders.

4) *Let them know you are praying.* Try to email, write or call once a week to let them know you are still praying for them.

5) *Hope and listen, and wait patiently with them.* People need a chance to be heard. Just listen. The words, "I can't feel God's presence," are frightening, and disheartening. Instead of giving answers to all their questions, try to reflect God's unconditional love for them. Standing quietly but firmly along–side someone, waiting with them, is to admit our own helplessness. It is an act of courage and hope. And like a good cry, talking it out makes hurting people feel a little better. Wait with them in spirit, and hope for them when they can't.

STEPS TOWARD INTERCESSORY PRAYER

Five parts of intercessory prayer are helpful to keep in mind as you engage in your prayer life.

1) *Pray for the world*—As this devotional is being written, there is continuing war in the Middle East. Much of the world is united to fight terrorism. Poverty rules significant portions of the globe. Pray for peace and comfort for the world.

2) *Pray for your nation*—Every day, leadership and the people they govern need prayer. Victims of difficulties from east to west, north and south benefit from prayer.

3) *Pray for your community*—What are the challenges facing your city's schools? Does everyone have a warm place to sleep at night? Is your church a leader in peace and justice issues, acting as the hands and feet of God? Your prayers will be an act of hope.

4) *Pray for persons close to you*—This may be your family, friends and co-workers. As busy as life can be, we must not be so busy that we are not praying for even those we're in touch with regularly and tangibly.

5) *Pray for yourself*—Again, this is not necessarily a selfish act, unless you are thinking of God as the Great Wish Granter, like asking the genie in the bottle for heart's desires. No, this is an act of self-care, drawing out the things in your heart you wish to talk to God about. Pray to mature in your faith, like growing, healthy vines bearing better and better fruit.

Acts of Hope Through Prayer Change Lives

Intercessory prayer is a sign for Christians that we are not alone in unsettling seasons of life. When others pray for us, alongside our own prayers, these acts move us closer to knowing God better. It also helps us to know each other better as we talk and listen to each other. Prayer, both offering it and seeking it, is an obstinate action to discover hope for those who have misplaced it.

Set a goal to maintain a regular prayer life. Listen for the needs of others to offer prayer on their behalf, whether they know it or not. Beware aware, also, of your own needs for prayer. Ask those you trust to pray for you, then add your needs to your prayer list—after you have remembered the world, your nation, your community and those close to you.

"Somebody's Praying Me Through" is a passionate testimony that intercessory prayer is the Christian community's powerful tool to bring hope to those who need it. It gives hope of being known and cared for by God, like that found in Psalm 139:14 "I will praise you, for I am fearfully and wonderfully made."

GREGORY RUMBURG
for Doxology Records

YOU SHALL REMEMBER THE LORD YOUR GOD,

FOR IT IS HE WHO GIVES YOU

POWER TO GET WEALTH, THAT HE MAY

ESTABLISH HIS COVENANT WHICH HE SWORE

TO YOUR FATHERS, AS IT IS THIS DAY.

—DEUTERONOMY 8:18

LET NOT THE FOUNDATION OF OUR HOPE

REST UPON MAN'S WISDOM. IT MUST BE FELT THAT

THERE IS NO NATIONAL SECURITY

BUT IN THE NATION'S HUMBLE, ACKNOWLEDGED

DEPENDENCE UPON GOD

AND HIS OVERRULING PROVIDENCE.

—PRESIDENT FRANKLIN PIERCE
in his inaugural address March 4, 1835

I LOOK TO THE GRACIOUS PROTECTION
OF THE DIVINE BEING WHOSE STRENGTHENING
SUPPORT I HUMBLY SOLICIT, AND WHOM
I FERVENTLY PRAY TO LOOK DOWN UPON US ALL.
MAY IT BE AMONG THE DISPENSATIONS
OF HIS PROVIDENCE TO BLESS OUR BELOVED
COUNTRY WITH HONORS AND WITH LENGTH
OF DAYS. MAY HER WAYS BE OF PLEASANTNESS
AND ALL HER PATHS BE PEACE!

—PRESIDENT MARTIN VAN BUREN
in his inaugural address March 4, 1837

Chapter Four

★ ★ ★

OUR NATION'S GODLY FUTURE

The past has been written. We see how our heritage is mostly bright, with some significant dark patches. We can learn from the past and apply those lessons in the present.

But the future has been written, too. All followers of Jesus know the end of the Book—after a period of unprecedented pain throughout the earth, God wins, Satan loses, and their disciples go to either glory or torment.

As individuals, we have to choose whether to work for the winning team or the losing team. If you're reading this book, you've probably committed your soul to Jesus. Praise God!

But how may the soul of a nation be committed? How can the United States of America achieve a godly future? There's only one way: Through the power of its people united in prayer and obedience.

Do all things without complaining and disputing, that you may become blameless and harmless, children of God without fault in the midst of a crooked and perverse generation, among whom you shine as lights in the world (Philippians 2:14–15).

Our nation was founded on Christian principles to be a beacon of freedom and hope in this world, but are Christians today thanked for sharing the light of Jesus? Often, no. Are we mocked, harmed, or even killed for our faith? Sometimes, yes, even in this country with its Constitutionally protected religious tolerance.

Remember . . .
This is the condemnation, that the light has come into the world, and men loved darkness rather than light, because their deeds were evil. For everyone practicing evil hates the light and does not come to the light, lest his deeds should be exposed (John 3:19–20).

Many of our citizens prefer the darkness, but our job as Christians is to persevere and to keep reflecting God's glory. We have to be "no matter what" people.

- If an election is coming up, pray for each candidate, not just the one you favor.
- If you don't agree with the leaders, pray for their wisdom to grow and for them to seek godly counsel.
- If you see dark fingers grasping for the heart of the nation, pray for the light of God to prosper.
- When you see beauty and goodness in the world, pray for God to multiply His blessings. Always remember what Jesus said: "You

have heard that it was said, 'You shall love your neighbor and hate your enemy.' But I say to you, love your enemies, bless those who curse you, do good to those who hate you, and pray for those who spitefully use you and persecute you, that you may be sons of your Father in heaven; for He makes His sun rise on the evil and on the good, and sends rain on the just and on the unjust" (Matthew 5:43–45). When you pray for a rain of blessings, ask that God will pour out His glory for everyone to treasure.

And no matter what, keep praying. Keep shining. And anticipate a godly future for the nation. God bless America! And America bless God!

The power of prayer is like turning on a light
as it illuminates God's purpose for our lives.
There is no greater connection to knowing His will other than the Word.
It is for this very reason that The Presidential Prayer Team *is needed.*

THOMAS KINKADE
Painter of Light™
& Honorary Committee Member
of *The Presidential Prayer Team*

THE ONLY HOPE FOR AMERICA

★　★　★

A woman and her husband, professing Christians, once asked me why I am an evangelist. "I long to see people changed by Jesus Christ," I replied. "That's my source of satisfaction."

She responded, "In my whole life I've never seen a person actually changed by Jesus Christ."

Her comment first touched my conscience. How changed am I by Jesus Christ? How different am I from my unchurched, unconverted neighbors?

Then I wanted to tell her about thousands of people I know whose lives have been dramatically changed: a drug dealer who once made thousands of dollars a week now content with his landscaping job that earns only hundreds a month; adulterous husbands and wives who now honor their marriage vows; lonely, withdrawn teenagers who now can't stop talking about Jesus at home and school; drug–addicted celebrities who now testify of deliverance and host Bible studies in their homes.

The resurrected Christ has power to change America, where eighty percent of the people claim to be Christians, but few live any differently from pagans or atheists, as though God has no claim on their lives. Their hearts have not been changed, and unless Jesus Christ changes their hearts, they never will be any different from those outside the Christian faith.

America needs evangelism like never before. Billy Graham once said, "It's either back to the Bible or back to the jungle." The jungle is creeping up on the United States.

Theologian Carl F. H. Henry put it this way: "The barbarians are coming." Dr. Henry could see that without a wave of evangelization that converts hundreds of thousands of people to Jesus Christ, barbarians are going to take over the land. Not foreigners, but our own unrepentant children and grandchildren.

The problem is in the heart, not just the outward behavior that so alarms and frightens God–fearing Americans. God says, "The heart is deceitful above all things, and desperately wicked" (Jeremiah 17:9). What's needed is not more good advice dished out in the newspaper and on television, but the Good News, "the power of God to salvation for everyone who believes" (Romans 1:16).

Political campaigns, family counseling, and education do nothing about the condition of human depravity. Unless there's a change of heart, nothing's happened to change a person. And unless millions of hearts are changed, little has happened to change America. Dr. Henry says, "The ideal way to transform a sinful society is not political compulsion but spiritual transformation, that is, evangelistic proclamation and regeneration."

If we proclaim the gospel with all the vigor of the Holy Spirit, I'm convinced hundreds of thousands, if not millions, of Americans will listen and trust Jesus Christ for salvation. That's America's only hope.

LUIS PALAU
President and Founder, Luis Palau Evangelistic Association
& Honorary Committee Member
of *The Presidential Prayer Team*

YOU ARE THE LIGHT OF THE WORLD.

A CITY THAT IS SET ON A HILL CANNOT BE HIDDEN.

NOR DO THEY LIGHT A LAMP AND

PUT IT UNDER A BASKET, BUT ON A LAMPSTAND,

AND IT GIVES LIGHT TO ALL WHO ARE IN THE

HOUSE. LET YOUR LIGHT SO SHINE

BEFORE MEN, THAT THEY MAY SEE YOUR

GOOD WORKS AND GLORIFY YOUR

FATHER IN HEAVEN.

—MATTHEW 5:14–16

Our Father and our God, we thank You for the many blessings You have poured out on America and we praise You for Your mercy. You have said: 'Righteousness exalts a nation, but sin is a disgrace to any people.' We confess, O Lord, our national and personal sins. We repent and ask forgiveness for all actions that dishonor You.

O God, bless our President and other leaders. Provide them with wisdom and move them to honor You. Deliver this great nation from all our enemies as we recommit ourselves to trust, serve and obey Your commands. We pray in the name of our Lord and Savior, Jesus Christ, Amen."

—DR. LUIS PALAU
National Day of Prayer, May 1, 2003

POLITICAL CONVICTIONS

"For this is the will of God, that by doing good
you may put to silence the ignorance of foolish men."
—1 Peter 2:15

★ ★ ★

When I first became a Christian, it was my conviction that politics was a corrupting influence and that Christianity and politics didn't mix.

However, as I look back over history, especially reading the early history of America, it's clear that Christianity and politics were intricately entwined—they were one and the same—and the religious convictions of our Founding Fathers are clear in everything they wrote: the Declaration of Independence, the Constitution, and the Bill of Rights.

So, now I'm more convinced that Christians must be involved in politics. I believe we have the responsibility to make our positions well–known. We have the right to vote for the candidates of our choice and to speak out against the candidates who don't stand for the value systems we hold dear.

If we don't get involved in politics, we will end up with exactly what we have today: a secular society. My spirit is grieved when I think of what we are leaving the generation of Americans who will follow us. Without the Christian foundation that was established in this country, we can easily become an evil society.

With a Christian foundation, we are God's unique creation and subject to God's unique blessings. So I would implore you to get involved. Pray about it and spend your money supporting candidates that best reflect your value system.

LARRY BURKETT
Founder and Chairman, Crown Financial Ministries
& Honorary Committee Member
of *The Presidential Prayer Team*

I SHALL LOOK FOR WHATEVER SUCCESS

MAY ATTEND MY PUBLIC SERVICE; AND KNOWING

THAT "EXCEPT THE LORD KEEP THE CITY

THE WATCHMAN WAKETH BUT IN VAIN," WITH

FERVENT SUPPLICATIONS FOR HIS FAVOR,

TO HIS OVERRULING PROVIDENCE I COMMIT WITH

HUMBLE BUT FEARLESS CONFIDENCE

MY OWN FATE AND THE FUTURE DESTINIES

OF MY COUNTRY.

—PRESIDENT JOHN QUINCY ADAMS
In his inaugural address March 4, 1825

THOUGHTS TO CONSIDER IN A TIME OF STRIFE

★ ★ ★

*W*e are moving rapidly into an age of extremes. We see it undeniably in acts of hatred, violence, intolerance and destruction. From the conflicts in the Middle East, we hear many reports of inhumanity. At the same time, we also see real heroes and the high cost of freedom. This is a battle against evil's assault on individual and national liberty. Love for others motivates the actions of our military and nation's leaders as surely as it moved Mother Teresa. Jesus stated clearly, "Greater love hath no man than this, that a man lay down his life for his friends" (John 15:13). Soldiers' sacrificial deeds express love undeniably. As we resist evil's threat in the Middle East and on the part of terrorists, we must also resist the evil that lurks in our own hearts. Evil always attacks that which is truly precious.

In all likelihood, it's only a matter of time before a direct assault comes once again to North America. My prayer is that before then we will witness extreme expressions of love, compassion, self–sacrifice, courage, strength of character, and unshakable resolve in our nation, which can only result from a genuine commitment to moral absolutes and the truth of Scripture.

Our nation must express more courage, conviction, and compassion than at any previous time in our history. The church must demonstrate godly love—even going beyond the sacrificial love exhibited by the early church in the book of Acts—to fulfill the challenge Jesus set forth in

Matthew 25 to meet the needs of "the least of these" through genuine concern and care.

We must not be deterred. Any attacks against us must deepen our resolve and strengthen our character. We must live according to biblical absolutes and be willing to give our lives before we would allow freedom to perish. If our nation does not move back toward absolute truth, I predict we will repeatedly experience firsthand the pain of unrestrained evil with its many horrors. Our decisions regarding the  absolutes and our attitude toward God, the source of life and true liberty, will determine the extent to which the horrors of evil will be felt within our borders. The forces of evil certainly will affect us, but whether or not they will destroy our way of life has yet to be determined.

The Middle East is a bomb with a rapidly burning fuse. Eventually the conflict there will result in Armageddon, as foretold in the book of Revelation. Jesus said there would be wars and rumors of wars in the last days.

The psalmist has said "our shield belongs to the LORD" (Psalm 89:18), and we must look to the Lord for our protection. That's why in an address to the nation early in 2002, President Bush encouraged people to pray for a shield of protection for our country, and that's why I believe so strongly that we must return to the absolutes in order to receive divine guidance.

The world already sees many radical expressions of hatred, vengeance, retaliation, and intolerance with all the ugly and devastating

LET US LEARN TOGETHER AND LAUGH TOGETHER

AND WORK TOGETHER AND PRAY TOGETHER,

CONFIDENT THAT IN THE END

WE WILL TRIUMPH TOGETHER IN THE RIGHT.

—PRESIDENT JIMMY CARTER

In his inaugural address, Jan. 20, 1977

consequences. It's time for all free nations to call Islamic leaders to account for their beliefs concerning people whom they consider infidels. Do they believe, as Mohammed declared shortly before his death, that the Jews and Christians must perish? Muslims in the United States expect protection, acceptance, and tolerance while enjoying the freedom and privilege they are afforded in this country; yet most Muslim countries offer no such benefits within their borders.

If enough Arab and Muslim leaders will courageously renounce extreme acts of terror and suicide bombings and begin to advocate good relationships with Israel and the West, then I believe there will be a period of peace.

If an easing of tensions does occur, then American and global businesses, the church, and the government of every free nation must move quickly to demonstrate a greater interest in the well–being of others. The strength of our alliances depends on how deeply the other nations value absolute principles that produce loyalty, commitment, honesty, and sacrifice. Our peace and security—and peace throughout the world—will be directly affected by our legitimate care and compassion for those who are less fortunate.

One Sunday, more than a year before the September 11 attacks, I was having lunch with a couple after speaking at their church. The wife asked me, "What do you believe will happen of significant importance in the United States and the world?"

I said that I anticipate great polarization in America. I believe we will tend to divide—liberal from conservative, good from evil, light from dark, selfish from holy, as many competing forces vie for our loyalty. However, Christians must refuse to polarize—we must penetrate all areas of life. Believers must not be drawn in to divisive movements; instead we must demonstrate unity as a model for others. There has never been a better time for the church of Jesus Christ to have a positive impact on the world.

This is the hour for all freedom–loving people to stand up and be counted. This is the time for people of compassion to begin to reach out all over the world. To all of my fellow Christian believers, to all who claim to have a personal relationship with Jesus Christ, if you have experienced the transforming power of what He referred to as "the spiritual new birth," you are going to hear God's call to commitment—not just commitment to national and world freedom and privilege as we have known it, but commitment to His eternal purposes.

The most powerful force available to stop the spread of deadly extremist ideologies is the love of God freely expressed through His people and through citizens who are compelled by compassion to reach out to the less privileged. Islamic extremists and other radical groups tend to flourish in areas of poverty and deep–seated human need, just as the Communists did in Eastern Europe, Russia, and Asia during the twentieth century.

Now more than ever, Christians must take the good news of Jesus Christ to the ends of the earth, proclaiming it in word and demonstrating it in deed. All Americans must seek ways to serve and to share with the less privileged in our own country and especially in developing nations. As we bless others, so shall be we blessed. The path to abundance of life is to give as freely as we have received.

Further, we must all assume responsibility for preserving the great privileges of freedom we enjoy in the United States by participating intelligently in the political process. We must make decisions based on principle, not preference or the personality of candidates. We must stand courageously and lovingly against the trends and beliefs that seek to undermine our freedoms. We must live in such a manner that people will be inspired by the undeniable characteristics and the positive results that are produced through our commitment to Jesus Christ and His commission.

We need the kind of commitment expressed by President Bush to my wife and me when we visited him in the Oval Office in spring 2001. During our conversation, I shared how it disturbed me to see him sometimes stereotyped as lacking in compassion. In response, the President leaned forward on the front edge of his chair and said firmly, "I do love people, and I want you to know I love the Lord, and I'm serious about my faith."

When I heard the leader of the free world affirm everything I had observed about him during the times he and I had prayed together over the past few years, I knew he had just voiced the key to the future hope of America: We must love people. We must love the Lord, and we must be serious about demonstrating our faith through acts of righteousness and compassion. These are attitudes and actions birthed in the hearts of those who properly respond to the absolutes.

It is time for all Christians and all freedom–loving Americans to rise up without fear and stand for truth. As King David says, "Even when I walk through the dark valley of death, I will not be afraid, for [God is] close beside me" (Psalm 23:4, NLT). The only way we will ever come to fear no evil and its deadly effect is if we know beyond a doubt that the Lord God Himself is with us, and we are with Him.

DR. JAMES ROBISON
President and Founder, LIFE Outreach International
& Honorary Committee Member
of *The Presidential Prayer Team*

AS WE MOVE FORWARD FROM SEPTEMBER 11,

LET US NOT SIMPLY FOCUS ON THE FUTURE IN AN

EFFORT TO FORGET THE PAST. LET US

REMEMBER WHO WE WERE ON SEPTEMBER 10 AND

THE EVENT THAT CHANGED ALL THAT. LET US

USE OUR DARKNESS TO BECOME PEOPLE OF DEEPER

CHARACTER, FAITH, AND LOVE. THIS WILL

THWART OUR ENEMIES AND HONOR OUR LOST

LOVED ONES IN A WAY NO

MEMORIAL OR TRIBUTE EVER COULD.

—LISA BEAMER

At the end of your life, you will never regret not having passed one more test, not winning one more verdict or not closing one more deal. You will regret time not spent with a husband, a friend, a child, or a parent. Fathers and mothers, if you have children . . . they must come first. You must read to your children, you must hug your children, you must love your children. Your success as a family . . . our success as a society . . . depends not on what happened at the White House, but on what happens inside your house.

—BARBARA BUSH

OH, GIVE THANKS TO THE LORD!

CALL UPON HIS NAME;

MAKE KNOWN HIS DEEDS AMONG THE PEOPLES!

SING TO HIM, SING PSALMS TO HIM;

TALK OF ALL HIS WONDROUS WORKS!

GLORY IN HIS HOLY NAME;

LET THE HEARTS OF THOSE REJOICE

WHO SEEK THE LORD!

SEEK THE LORD AND HIS STRENGTH;

SEEK HIS FACE EVERMORE!

—PSALM 105:1–4

May that Being who is supreme over all, the Patron of Order, the Fountain of Justice, and the Protector in all ages of the world of virtuous liberty, continue His blessing upon this nation and its Government and give it all possible success and duration consistent with the ends of His providence.

—PRESIDENT JOHN ADAMS
In his inaugural address, March 4, 1797

I CAN EXPRESS NO BETTER HOPE

FOR MY COUNTRY THAN THAT THE KIND

PROVIDENCE WHICH SMILED UPON OUR FATHERS

MAY ENABLE THEIR CHILDREN TO PRESERVE THE

BLESSINGS THEY HAVE INHERITED.

—President Franklin Pierce
In his inaugural address, March 4, 1835

I WILL PRAY FOR THE LEADERS OF TODAY . . . AND TOMORROW

★ ★ ★

*I*nspirational thoughts about prayer and its benefits are useless unless the action of prayer follows those thoughts.

Is prayer a good idea? Yes.

Is it part of our national heritage? Of course.

Does it make a difference in our hearts, homes, nation, and world? Absolutely.

Is our nation's future dependent upon prayer? Without a doubt.

So what's stopping you? Do it. Pray! Now!

Our President needs wisdom to handle the burdens of office and to make decisions that benefit this country and God's Kingdom.

Members of the Cabinet, Congress, Supreme Court, and other leadership positions need to rely on and provide godly counsel in all matters that come before them.

In the often-overlooked local elections, you and your neighbors must choose who will lead your community. Will it be someone motivated by selfishness or someone motivated by service?

Pray today for tomorrow's leaders. Next time you see children playing, pray that they develop godly character and that they cherish godly principles for living. Take note of what the children are learning, and pray that they grow in appropriate knowledge and wisdom. Pray that as they learn how to work and play well with others, they develop relationship skills that will serve them—and their communities—as they become the leaders America needs.

Commit to praying for this nation, and you will see God's glory reflected in its people like never before.

If you're unsure of what exactly to pray, visit www.presidentialprayerteam.org for updates on particular issues, or just look out your window. Opportunity and need are everywhere.

Pray. Just pray.

TRUST IN THE LORD WITH ALL YOUR HEART,

AND LEAN NOT ON YOUR OWN UNDERSTANDING;

IN ALL YOUR WAYS ACKNOWLEDGE HIM,

AND HE SHALL DIRECT YOUR PATHS.

DO NOT BE WISE IN YOUR OWN EYES;

FEAR THE LORD AND DEPART FROM EVIL.

IT WILL BE HEALTH TO YOUR FLESH,

AND STRENGTH TO YOUR BONES.

HONOR THE LORD WITH YOUR POSSESSIONS,

AND WITH THE FIRSTFRUITS OF ALL YOUR INCREASE;

SO YOUR BARNS WILL BE FILLED WITH PLENTY,

AND YOUR VATS WILL OVERFLOW WITH NEW WINE.

—PROVERBS 3:5–10

ABOUT THE PRESIDENTIAL
PRAYER TEAM

★ ★ ★

*A*fter the terrorist attacks on September 11, 2001, the President of the United States asked all Americans to pray. *The Presidential Prayer Team* was birthed less than a week later. Since then, millions have answered the call to the President and many have joined *The Presidential Prayer Team*, receiving regular email updates on the President's prayer needs. Anyone can join. Membership is free. Join by visiting www.presidentialprayerteam.org or www.presidentialprayerkids.org for children.

The Presidential Prayer Team is a spiritual movement of the American people that is not affiliated with any political party or official. It gains no direction or support, official or unofficial, from the current administration, from any agency of the government or from any political party, so that it may be free and unencumbered to equally serve the prayer needs of all current and future leaders of our great nation.

The Presidential Prayer Team seeks the involvement of all Americans who are committed to pray for the President, crossing ethnic, political, and religious backgrounds for the benefit of the nation. It holds no affiliation with any political or religious organizations, nor will the organization ever be used for political purposes.

PRESIDENTIAL PRAYER TEAM
STATEMENT OF FAITH

*(adopted from the Mission America Coalition,
www.missionamerica.org)*

We believe in the Holy Scriptures as originally given by God, divinely inspired, infallible, entirely trustworthy; and the supreme authority in all matters of faith and conduct.

2 PETER 1:20, 21; 2 TIMOTHY 3:15–17; JOHN 17:17;
MATTHEW 5:17,18

We believe in One God, eternally existent in three persons, Father, Son and Holy Spirit.

DEUTERONOMY 6:4; 1 TIMOTHY 1:17;
MATTHEW 28:19; 2 CORINTHIANS 13:14

We believe in our Lord Jesus Christ, God manifest in the flesh, His virgin birth, His sinless human life, His divine miracles, His vicarious and atoning death, His bodily resurrection, His ascension, His mediatorial work and His personal imminent return in power and glory.

COLOSSIANS 2:9; JOHN 1:1; GALATIANS 4:4; MATTHEW
1:23; HEBREWS 4:15; ACTS 2:22,23; 1 PETER 3:18;
COLOSSIANS 2:13,14: 2 CORINTHIANS 5:21; 1 JOHN 1:7;
1 CORINTHIANS 15:4; MARK 16: 9; ROMANS 8:34;
HEBREWS 7:25; MATTHEW 24:30

We believe in God the Holy Spirit, by whose indwelling the believer is enabled to live a holy life, and to witness and work for the Lord Jesus Christ.

ACTS 5:3,4; ROMANS 8:9–11; ROMANS 8:12–14; GALATIANS 5:16–25; ACTS 1:8; MATTHEW 10:19,20; JOHN 14:26; 15:26,27

We believe in the Salvation of lost and sinful people through the shed blood of the Lord Jesus Christ by grace alone through faith, apart from works and by regeneration of the Holy Spirit.

1 PETER 3:18; EPHESIANS 2:8,9; 1 JOHN 1:8 – 2:2; ROMANS 3:21–26; TITUS 3:4–7

We believe in the unity of Spirit of all true believers, which comprises the Church, the Body of Christ.

JOHN 17: 20–23; EPHESIANS 2:12–22

We believe in the mission of the Church to go to all the world and make disciples of all nations.

MATTHEW 28:18–20; LUKE 24: 45–47; ACTS 2:8

We believe in the Resurrection of both the saved and the lost: they that are saved unto the resurrection of life, they that are lost unto the resurrection of damnation.

1 CORINTHIANS 15: 20–26; 42–44; JOHN 5:21–29; 1 JOHN 5:10–12; REVELATION 20:11–15

For I know the thoughts that I think toward you, says the Lord, thoughts of peace and not of evil, to give you a future and a hope. Then you will call upon Me and go and pray to Me, and I will listen to you. And you will seek Me and find Me, when you search for Me with all your heart. I will be found by you, says the LORD.

—JEREMIAH 29:11–14

Again I say to you that if two of you agree on earth concerning anything that they ask, it will be done for them by My Father in heaven. For where two or three are gathered together in My name, I am there in the midst of them.

—MATTHEW 18:19–20

The first day that you set your heart to understand, and to humble yourself before your God, your words were heard

—DANIEL 10:12

If you abide in Me, and My words abide in you, you will ask what you desire, and it shall be done for you.

—JOHN 15:7

Be anxious for nothing, but in everything by prayer and supplication, with thanksgiving, let your requests be made known to God; and the peace of God, which surpasses all understanding, will guard your hearts and minds through Christ Jesus.

—PHILIPPIANS 4:6–7

Confess your trespasses to one another, and pray for one another, that you may be healed. The effective, fervent prayer of a righteous man avails much.

—JAMES 5:16

If My people who are called by My name will humble themselves, and pray and seek My face, and turn from their wicked ways, then I will hear from heaven, and will forgive their sin and heal their land.

—2 CHRONICLES 7:14

The sacrifice of the wicked is an abomination to the LORD,
But the prayer of the upright is His delight.

—PROVERBS 15:8

SCRIPTURES ABOUT PRAYER

★ ★ ★

Rejoice always, pray without ceasing, in everything give thanks; for this is the will of God in Christ Jesus for you.

—1 THESSALONIANS 5:16–18

The Holy Spirit helps us in our distress. For we don't even know what we should pray for, nor how we should pray. But the Holy Spirit prays for us with groanings that cannot be expressed in words.

—ROMANS 8:26 (NLT)

The LORD is my rock and my fortress
   and my deliverer;
My God, my strength, in whom I will
   trust;
My shield and the horn of my salvation, my stronghold.
I will call upon the Lord, who is worthy to be praised;
So shall I be saved from my enemies.

—PSALM 18:2–3

Hear a just cause, O LORD,
Attend to my cry;
Give ear to my prayer which is not
   from deceitful lips.

—PSALM 17:1

For this reason we also, since the day we heard it, do not cease to pray for you, and to ask that you may be filled with the knowledge of His will in all wisdom and spiritual understanding; that you may walk worthy of the Lord, fully pleasing Him, being fruitful in every good work and increasing in the knowledge of God; strengthened with all might, according to His glorious power, for all patience and longsuffering with joy;

—COLOSSIANS 1:9–11

And this I pray, that your love may abound still more and more in knowledge and all discernment, that you may approve the things that are excellent, that you may be sincere and without offense till the day of Christ.

—PHILIPPIANS 1:9–10

Now to Him who is able to do exceedingly abundantly above all that we ask or think, according to the power that works in us, to Him be glory in the church by Christ Jesus to all generations, forever and ever. Amen.

—EPHESIANS 3:20–21

Days to Keep in Prayer

★ ★ ★

Federal Holidays

★ ★ ★

New Year's Day . . . . January 1
Martin Luther King, Jr., Day . . . . Third Monday in January
Presidents Day . . . . Third Monday in February
Memorial Day . . . . Final Monday in May
Independence Day . . . . July 4
Labor Day . . . . First Monday in September
Columbus Day . . . . Second Monday in October
Veterans Day . . . . November 11
Thanksgiving Day . . . . Fourth Thursday in November
Christmas Day . . . . December 25

National Observances

★ ★ ★

National Day of Prayer . . . . First Thursday in May
Mother's Day . . . . Second Sunday in May
Father's Day . . . . Third Sunday in June
Juneteenth (Liberation of Slaves) . . . . . June 19
Grandparents' Day . . . . Sunday after Labor Day
Patriot Day . . . . September 11
Citizenship or Constitution Day . . . . . September 17
National Children's Day . . . . Second Sunday in October

Please check www.presidentialprayerteam.org for updates about other times of urgent prayer, and be observant for information about local and national elections that also need to be covered in prayer.

Now it shall come to pass, if you diligently obey the voice of the LORD your God, to observe carefully all His commandments which I command you today, that the Lord your God will set you high above all nations of the earth. And all these blessings shall come upon you and overtake you, because you obey the voice of the Lord your God . . . Then all peoples of the earth shall see that you are called by the name of the Lord, and they shall be afraid of you. And the Lord will grant you plenty of goods, in the fruit of your body, in the increase of your livestock, and in the produce of your ground, in the land of which the Lord swore to your fathers to give you. The Lord will open to you His good treasure, the heavens, to give the rain to your land in its season, and to bless all the work of your hand. You shall lend to many nations, but you shall not borrow . . . But it shall come to pass, if you do not obey the voice of the Lord your God, to observe carefully all His commandments and His statutes which I command you today, that all these curses will come upon you and overtake you . . . The Lord will send on you cursing, confusion, and rebuke in all that you set your hand to do, until you are destroyed and until you perish quickly, because of the wickedness of your doings in which you have forsaken Me.

—DEUTERONOMY 28:1–2, 10–12, 15, 20

ACKNOWLEDGMENTS

★ ★ ★

Grateful acknowledgment is made to the following publishers for permission to reprint this copyrighted material.

pp. 50-51   Stormie Omartian, *The Power of a Praying Nation* (Eugene, Oregon: Harvest House Publishers, 2002).

pp. 58-62   Franklin Graham, *The Name* (Nashville: Thomas Nelson, 2002).

pp. 64-65   Lisa Beamer, *Let's Roll* (Wheaton, Illinois: Tyndale House, 2002).

p. 66   "There She Stands," Written by Michael W. Smith and Wes King © 2002 World Music, Inc./SmittyFly Music (admin. by Word Music, Inc.)/ASCAP/Lotterthanme Music/ASCAP.

p. 69   "Stand," Written by Rebecca St. James and Reggie Hamm © 2000 Up In the Mix Music / Bibbitsong Music (BMI)/ Designer Music, Inc. / Minnie Partners Music / McSpadden–Smith Music (SESAC).

pp. 82-83   © 2003 Joni Eareckson Tada

pp. 90-91   Woodrow Kroll, *When God Doesn't Answer* (Grand Rapids: Baker Book House Company, 1997).

pp. 102-107   Gregory Rumburg, "Acts of Hope: A Devotional Based on 'Somebody's Praying Me Through'" <www.doxologyrecords.com> 14 May 2003.

pp. 114-115   Copyright © 2003 by Luis Palau. Excerpted from *The Only Hope for America* (Crossway Books, 1996). Used with permission. All rights reserved.

pp. 118-119   Larry Burkett, *Great Is Thy Faithfulness* (Ulrichsville, Ohio: Promise Press, an imprint of Barbour Publishing, Inc., 1998)

pp. 120-125   James Robison, *The Absolutes: Freedom's Only Hope* (Wheaton, Illinois: Tyndale House, 2002).

IT MUST BE FELT THAT THERE IS

NO NATIONAL SECURITY

BUT IN THE NATION'S HUMBLE

ACKNOWLEDGED DEPENDENCE UPON GOD

AND HIS OVERRULING PROVIDENCE.

—PRESIDENT JOHN ADAMS